CHARLIE'S WAR

CHARLIE'S WAR

By

**Flg. Officer
CHARLES H MATTHEWS
(RAFVR Rtd.)**

Date of Publication:
May 1998

Published by:
Charles H. Matthews

© Copyright 1998 Charles H. Matthews

Printed by:
ProPrint
Riverside Cottage
Great North Road
Stibbington
Peterborough PE8 6LR

ISBN: 0 9532860 0 2

CONTENTS:

                                                          PAGE NO:

CHAPTER 1.	Across the Bay	1
CHAPTER 2.	Initial training	9
CHAPTER 3.	Advanced training	28
CHAPTER 4.	Over the desert to Cairo	36
CHAPTER 5.	Training for the job	44
CHAPTER 6.	Posted overseas	55
CHAPTER 7.	Ferrying to the Gold Coast	58
CHAPTER 8.	Conversions to more types	65
CHAPTER 9.	Promotions and Prangs	69
CHAPTER 10.	Christmas in Blida	74
CHAPTER 11.	Busy in Italy	81
CHAPTER 12.	Four engines and drop the Lifeboat	91
CHAPTER 13.	The War ends, return to England	101
CHAPTER 14	Worlds apart, Sports day in Udine	114
CHAPTER 15.	Contretemps at Melton and Paris	126
CHAPTER 16.	Home posting and Customs	137
CHAPTER 17.	A new squadron and a voyage to India	147
CHAPTER 18.	Cook's tours, Vip's and baggage	161
CHAPTER 19.	RAFVR, and the Korean war, I fly for my country again.	173

The experiences and diary of a Transport command pilot, during the war in North Africa and Italy. How we moved the aircraft to the forward areas of combat, unarmed, with a minimum of crew, in spite of the elements, plus the 'do not hazard the aircraft' edict, and enjoyed the pleasure of flying as many types of the aircraft as was allowable. To all my companions in No. 3 Aircraft Delivery Unit, and No. 3 Ferry Unit, 216 Group, Middle East Command, I dedicate this story. I had to put the record straight.

Charlie's War

The diary of an RAF Transport Pilot

PREFACE

At the dusk of my life and suffering the plague of disability and arthritis I have decided to relate this account of my war-time memories on behalf of all the Transport Command Air crews whose works, to my knowledge, have gone unrecorded.

I began to write this story several months ago when encouraged by my friends Terry Clark and Bill Graham at the local Shopmobility unit, in Coventry, the city in which I grew up, and where I remained with my family after my war service in the Royal Air Force.

I have shared with them my experiences of flying for the RAF during the Second World War and my undiminished enthusiasm for flying, when even today, given the opportunity to go onto the flight deck of a passenger jet, sometimes requesting a visit through a stewardess, I jump at the chance, metaphorically, such is my love of aeroplanes. The seeds of this love affair with flight, were sown when I was at school way back in the 1920's and 30's when I read every piece of news and followed the press, on their accounts of the developments in new aeroplanes being produced throughout the aviation world, both British and foreign. The recorded exploits of the RFC pilots were devoured with the insatiable pleasure of youth and naiveté, without knowledge of the outcome of aerial warfare both to the airmen and the civilians caught up in the madness of war.

That I survived the Coventry Blitz attacks in 1940 was more power to my resolve, that led me to decide what my future involvement would be in those maniacal years, when man made all the same mistakes of all previous wars and defamed his own intelligence.

Terry and Bill are both avid fans of the aircraft of the period of the war years and immediately post war, whether friend or foe. Thus from the chats we have in the Shopmobility 'cabin,' to these two new friends, I am indebted for their generous encouragement, and the aide-memoirs to the past, which unlocked the gates and drew aside the veils of clouded recollections to bring back to life, those difficult yet exhilarating days in the skies of Europe, Canada and the Mediterranean area, and of the conflict with the forces of Germany.

Those memorable days when we trained, flew and maybe, died, as teenagers or at most very young men, are gone forever but cannot nor should not be erased from the histories of those brave boys, close friends forever, no matter what the morrow brought.

      Charles H. Matthews
      Coventry 1997.

CHAPTER ONE

Now we can start, as the throttles open we cannot believe our luck that we'll soon be away from this place, the time is ten pm on the eleventh of March 1944. We rise off the runway after a longer roll than usually because of the extra weight of the fuel load. There are three hundred gallons of extra fuel in the bomb-bay tank to give the long range required for this our first ferry flight. The controller gives me the clearance to leave the circuit and set course for our destination in North Africa.

It would be easy to be complacent over the flight ahead. We all knew of the dangers and problems to be faced, especially when we turned south over the Bay of Biscay, the enemy would be fairly close, and without armament or crew to man them we would be a sitting duck, if caught out too near the French coast, or for that matter the Channel Islands.

We settled into our routines, and set out our procedures as if still on Training exercises at OTU. The Scillies would be our first way mark, here we were to finally check all systems satisfactory, before proceeding. Here also, I would make the change to use the bomb-bay overload tank. The only possible diversion other than a return to England early on, would be to Gibraltar in the later part of the flight, however they were in the midst of an outbreak of Smallpox, and although we had had the jabs for overseas service, and a vaccination before leaving Hurn, we did not wish to risk landing at Gib. Our destination was Rabat, in Morocco, getting on for eight hours away, some fifteen hundred miles, across the Bay of Biscay, on to the south of Portugal, then across the eastern Atlantic ocean. After an hour or so, we were told by the navigator that we should be over the Isles of Scilly. Now we must put into practise the lessons learned at Melton Mowbray when being trained for the operation ahead of us. I called the orders to my crew to commence the fuel change over.

Two years in training to get to this point and still I had seen no action and was not likely to do so. It had been long and tedious; learning to fly was not so onerous as I had expected; it was the disciplines Navigation, Signals, Survival and escape, Photography, Morse Code, Gunnery, Aircraft Recognition, Ship Recognition etc. etc. that demanded most of one's attention. The long hours in classes learning, memorising, examinations, plus the ogre of the dreaded Washout hanging over one's head all of the waking hours. Then finally, the greatest ignominy of all, to spend interminable weeks at some holding unit while some boffin, or desk-wallah, decides where your talents will finally be tested. So here we are at last six thousand feet above the Scilly Isles in a brand new Wellington Mark 10, serial No. LP 145, to deliver to Middle East Command in Cairo, for onward ferrying, not that we knew our destination at this time. Our problems were about to begin.

Frank Allaire, my French Canadian wireless air gunner went back, climbing over the main spar to reach the fuel cocks, which he would set to transfer from the overload tank in the bomb bay to the engine supply lines. This required first to select the tank and prime the lines, then, when I had turned on the booster pumps, the fuel should flow to the engines and the normal tank cocks could be turned off. He gave me the nod 'All set,' I turn off the port main tank cock, then a short wait to check that fuel was flowing, the port engine began to splutter, I quickly turned on the cross feed and called to Frank to recheck his settings and reprime the lines.

That done, it was off with the cross feed and wait, until again shortly afterwards the engine began to play-up, so it was cross feed back on then over to main again. Throughout this time we circled over the way mark using our precious fuel to no good purpose trying both engines, and all possible combinations of fuel cocks, cross feed, pumps etc. until after twenty minutes had gone by on this fruitless task, I had to decide whether to go on or abort.

I conferred with Dennis Cooke, my Navigator, over the estimated flight time, deciding what would be a suitable height at which to fly, what options we had for going to Gibraltar should we be forced to, against our previous decision to avoid the place. He checked from the gauges how much fuel still remained, from this he could calculate the safety margin to be expected. He came through soon with the information, that we should have a surplus of an hour. This was enough! The die was cast when I turned on to the new course.

I had been flying on manual since Hurn and at last was able to engage the Auto-pilot and get out of the seat to stretch. Since it was early March it was still very cold at height and all three crew were wearing full kit which made movement difficult, but when I reduced our height to three thousand feet, for the best economical fuel consumption, it would be better as the heaters would be more efficient. Returning to the pilot's seat I began the descent by setting the control trim tabs to lose height very gradually over about half an hour, at this setting of the 'trims' we would have covered extra miles, due to the increased airspeed so reducing the relative fuel consumption. More fuel would be left for the later part of the flight.

The long haul across the Bay was in total darkness one of the darkest nights I could remember, because of total cloud cover and no moon. Frank was supplying radio-bearings for Dennis but these became less accurate as we flew south, since the only airfields we were able to contact were those in Cornwall and it was not possible to obtain an intersecting bearing, we only knew of our direction in relationship to say St. Eval. Not until we could receive the Spanish commercial stations and were able to identify them could we hope to do better, it would have to be dead reckoning for the present, and our hope was that a series of fixes would be possible, using the Spanish Lighthouses along the coast from Cape Finisterre down to Portugal and on south to Cape St. Vincent.

However back to flying across the Bay on this pitch black night, relying totally on instruments, checking and rechecking the auto-pilot, since this version was really only an aid to the pilot to ease the workload and not particularly efficient. How is the rate of descent, is the course correct? Check the compass, check engine settings, boost pressure, pitch settings, engine revs. oil pressure and temperature, until the monotony gets to you and you start to drift into thought.

Way, way back in 1941 when I tried to join this man's Air Force I thought that I could set the world to rights, get qualified and shoot the Hun out of the skies. How wrong can one be! The changing policies of the

Leaders, even Churchill himself, would reshape the needs for trained air crews. Bomber Harris wanted his fair share to carry out his heavy bombardment using Bomber Command. There was another war going on in the Middle East, where Rommel was making things very hard for the Eighth Army and the squadrons supporting them. I wasn't a born fighter, all I wanted to do was fly and on the way try to 'do my bit' for the war effort instead of wasting my time behind a desk.

I started in the usual way, going into the recruiting office in the Sibree Hall in Coventry, in June, where a Sgt. in the RAF wanted to know why I was here and what trade I wanted to train in. I of course replied 'Pilot.' I was interviewed as to my education. My School certificate grades seemed to swing things, then I had a basic medical followed by a discussion, as to what my job was at Armstrong Whitworth, and if it was of such importance that I should stay in what was referred to as a reserved occupation. I claimed tongue in cheek, that the extent of my work was to file drawings and make tea for the older and senior draughtsmen. They the RAF in the shape of the recruiting Sergeant, believed it, so I was given the OK, and accepted, then told I was to wait for a few days, to await my orders as to which Selection Board I would report.

This selection testing took place in Birmingham and after being through the mill all day at interviews, tests in maths, geography, and aptitude testing on funny bits of strange kit, which were to test one's reactions etc. Then medical and eye tests of a strenuous nature, I was quizzed as to my reasons for wanting to fly with the

RAF, I gave some weird and wonderful reply which I cannot remember and satisfied the senior officer present.

I left with the King's two half crowns, the statutory signing on fee, and an RAF Volunteer Reserve Badge, to wait for the notice detailing when and where to report. From June to October I fretted away at work, wishing my life away in my anxiety to 'get cracking' and start my training. I duly reported one fine October morning to the Aircrew Reception Centre at Lords cricket ground in Abbey Road, St. John's Wood, London. ACRC it was known as, what a mouthful!

Here we were shorn of all inhibitions, lost our civvy identity, became a number and learned the devious ways of service life. As an innocent abroad in the capital, up from the country I soon grasped the way of the world, where dog eats dog and the strong rule the roost. I disliked corporals intensely, they treated us like dirt, they tried to humiliate us at every opportunity, and we became as mean as them or worse if that was possible. We would skive off at weekends to go home even for a few hours, then return overnight on the train to arrive on Monday morning at about five and attempt to avoid these same corporals as we climbed through the back windows of the apartments we occupied in St. Johns Wood Road.

The ride up to Coventry on the train from Euston, when I had weekend trips home from ACRC, was often a case of standing all the way in the main corridor or the vestibule at the entrance to the carriage. The trains were always packed out especially with troops on the move on postings or leave, the red crimson locomotives of the LMS stand out in my memories and when waiting at Coventry for the midnight return train I had an interest in the names of the locos. The Euston bound train arrived in London at about two thirty am or maybe a little later and I had to run the gauntlet of the Military Police who were always on the lookout for absentees, the Naafi had a small hut where it sold tea and wads, before finding a suitable bench to kip on until the Underground started up around five in the morning. One of the preferred resting places was the mantel shelves over the big hot water radiators in the famous Grand hall of Euston station. Then at Avenue Road or Swiss Cottage underground stations it was the MP's again whom we had to avoid since these trips were always without passes.

Opposite our billets was the London Zoological Gardens, each morning and evening we marched along to the dining hall on the zoo site where RAF cooks tried to outdo each other in attempting to ruin good food. If anyone was due for punishment, it usually entailed going to the cookhouse and being made to clean pans or peel spuds. One crazy thing about marching to meals was the fact that as it was winter, the mornings were very dark so an airman of the front rank and the rear rank on the outside file carried a paraffin burning hurricane lamp the front white and the rear a red light, it was too comical, for all the world like a caterpillar trying to emulate a railway train.

Several weeks on, I found myself in Brighton at the Metropole Hotel in a holding unit, the pipe line had become choked with trainees, and the winter weather had caused problems at the Flying Schools, delaying the finishing of many courses. I was spending my first Christmas away from my home and family little did I know at that time that this was to become the pattern for years to come.

CHAPTER TWO

The initial Training Wing I was sent to was No. 8 at Newquay in Cornwall, here the RAF had commandeered all the hotels for the duration of hostilities, to establish a training regime in which all young and not so young Aircrew went, effectively back to school. We studied Airforce Law as it applied to airmen. Morse code signalling with both the radio transmitters, and also the Aldis lamp, sending messages to our opposite group who were posted at the other side of the bay. Every morning we paraded on the road outside our hotel come rain or shine, when wet we wore the infamous ground sheet which doubled up as a raincoat of sorts, equally every day we were marched to the car park opposite the church, were the drill corporal delighted in drilling us until we nearly dropped. What useful purpose it served in pilot training I never found out, but drill we did all through the Winter and into Spring. There were also lessons in how to disassemble and assemble a water cooled Lewis machine gun and its mate the Vickers, ask any service man what he knows about machine guns and he will repeat like a zombie, something about the rear sear retainer keeper and its spring. How that useless bit of information would be put to good use only them upstairs would know, in all my service career I was not to meet this thing again. Physical education was done on the beach when the tide was conveniently out, or on the grassy area on the cliff tops near the billets. My room looked out to the little island on the town beach with the famous little suspension bridge crossing the gap, all the postcards have that view of Newquay, amazingly they called our hotel the Beachview I wonder why?

Newquay had its good points, we struck up a camaraderie with others of the flight to which we were assigned which lasted through thick and thin, we would lie for each other, do duty shifts for one another or cover in those times when things went wrong. After twelve weeks we were supposed to have completed the course, and quite a large number of our flight were sent onward to the next part of training. Myself and several others were held back to form what became known as X flight, and it became apparent later that we were all married men. Coincidence or not we had a period of six or seven weeks lazing in the sunny Spring weather of the beautiful Cornish coast. One task we were given was the repainting of the underwater surfaces of the sail boat that the RAF used to demonstrate Navigation to the pupils. Since it was only possible to paint at low tide we had to make arrangements to be available, at short notice to wade out into the harbour and shore up the boat and get the bottom scraped. The job lasted well into May, with the fine weather it was a life of Riley for many weeks. The stores kitted us out with flying gear at Newquay plus the extra kit bag to carry it all in and of course the mandatory photographs were taken in full flying suits, to send home to family and wives or girlfriends. I had a week on leave in April and my girl friend and I were married at our local church, St. George's in Coundon, where I had been the Rover Scout Leader, my very good friend George Bennett was the vicar who performed the ceremony. There was to be no honeymoon that would have to wait, I left for camp in 48 hrs. after the wedding.

The train journey back to Newquay was typical of conditions on the railways of war time Britain grossly overcrowded with troops on the move mostly going on or coming back from leave. I had to leave from Coventry station at about eight pm on a Sunday night to travel to Birmingham where in a grimy and smoky New street station I made my way onto the over bridge to change from one platform to another. I was to go on the Bristol train via Cheltenham and Gloucester, on the old Midland line. The station was a hive of activity, Service men and women returning to their units, on the platform were couples saying goodbye to one another, and the Military Police patrolling the area were having a field day checking on passes or the lack thereof. But the major memory was of the forces standing three or four deep, on the platform edge, waiting for the train to come in. When it did finally arrive the doors opened and a host of bodies came pouring out to fight their way through the massed throng on the platform, then the scramble to get into the coaches and find a seat. A seat if you were lucky, and some huge sailor did not depose you, and you were ending up in the corridor which was also packed out, mostly standing room only. The air was thick with cigarette smoke and the smell of sweating bodies and sandwiches and booze, anything went on those journeys. To visit the toilet was an obstacle course of climbing over bodies, kit bags, suitcases, etc. the chance that if you did have a seat when you started your trip along the carriage it would be gone on your return, then the problem of ejecting the persons who were occupying the toilet as a travelling seat. A nightmare scene.

At Bristol our troubles were still not over, there was a wait between train connections at Temple Meads of around an hour, it was a short step across the concourse between platforms to find the correct one for the London to Penzance train. There was even enough time to stand in the queue for a cup of tea at the NAAFI counter and of course it was now nearing midnight, and it appeared that the whole of the Royal Navy was on the station, there were so many sailors around. I suppose that this station was a focal point for the connections from the north. They were heading for the dockyard at Plymouth and a return to their ship. The train duly arrived, panting with the enormous load it was pulling, there were probably about fifteen carriages on the back and all seemed to be full with people standing in every conceivable space. In fact when I got on board, I found there were lightweight guys lying up on the luggage shelves, over the heads of the seated passengers.

So down the line through Bridgewater, Taunton, and into Exeter where at least some dismounted and the rest breathed a bit easier. Finally we arrived at Plymouth in the early hours of Monday morning, and heaven; we had acres of seats to ourselves, the Navy left us together with their rubbish and empty beer bottles to continue over the Saltash bridge into Cornwall on our way to Par where I was to change yet again for Newquay.

However all was not plain sailing in these tempestuous days, for did I not arrive on the cold deserted platform at Par station at four in the morning, and have yet another wait for the first train out to Newquay at six thirty am. I recall that with a friend on a previous occasion we turned up at a house in Par to stay the night after a recommendation by the station master as to where to find lodgings. We had arrived there on an earlier train, but too late for the last train connection and had an all night wait until morning. The first train into Newquay would get travellers there in time for first parade at eight o'clock, unfed and the worse for wear after the long journey. Had it not been for the generous hospitality of the lady in Par, I and two friends would have been in the silly situation of failing to be on parade in the correct dress and in a clean and smart order.

I was due to be posted to a Grading School, the orders came through near the end of May. I had to travel to Reading to the Reserve Flying School at Woodley, for assessment as to suitability for further training as a pilot. The Empire Flying Training Scheme was very expensive in cost to run, both in men and machines, therefore a system of checking a pupil's potential for flying were assessed before the long journey out to Canada, or South Africa, or Rhodesia was made. The trainee pilots were given training up to solo stage, and did a course of fifteen hours flying on, Tiger Moths or in my case the Miles Magister monoplane trainer. This was a delightful aeroplane to fly. I 'went solo' after twelve hours instruction and a big problem to resolve, I was prone to air sickness. It first came to light on the second or third trip with my instructor, who incidentally was a tower of strength. I could have lost out there and then, but he insisted that I visit the Medical Officer for treatment. The Mo's remedy was a thick milky liquid which I had to take ten minutes before taking to the air, and it worked, by the seventh flight I was fine and over the problem, so we stopped the treatment and I never looked back from then on.

Going solo is the first challenge to a raw pilot and is one of the memorable moments to savour, you have a tremendous sense of exhilaration, no fear that you are on your own, because you have earned it the hard way, through diligence and practise, listening and watching all that the instructor was able to show you.

The Final assessment by the O.C. Flying, W/Cmdr Moir, was <u>Average</u> and fit to continue training and to proceed to further training at Elementary Flying Training School.

On the fourth of June 1942 I left Woodley to report to Heaton Park in Manchester, to an embarkation unit, for preparations for the voyage overseas. Leaving Woodley, No. 8 E.F.T.S. on June 9th, I took seven days overseas embarkation leave at home trying to console the family and went up to Heaton Park, where all our flying kit, Gas masks, ground sheets, anti-gas equipment and other paraphernalia relating to service in a war zone as England then was, was handed in to the stores, as they were not necessary for overseas postings, we even turned in our boots that had received such slavish treatment, to gain the shine beloved of sergeants, and were issued instead with shoes, two pairs in fact. From Manchester, having been separated from our main kit bag, to travel in the ship's hold, we left with our backpacks for the journey. We went in a convoy of trucks to the railway station, travelling to Gourock on the Clyde, where, with many others I embarked on the former refrigerator ship S.S. Letitia bound for Canada.

After five most unpleasant days on the Atlantic suffering from sea sickness for almost the entire journey; sleeping in swaying hammocks which we had to rig each night and clear each morning, then being force fed by my friend Jim Standen, to ward off the sickness; I saw the lights of Halifax, Nova Scotia on the horizon. When we started off from Scotland, we had an escort of three destroyers, the orders from the bridge were that no lights should be showing at night, that it was taboo to use electric razors, since the sparking of the brushes on the motors was causing radio interference. On the second day out one of the destroyers turned south and was not seen again, then on the fourth day we found we were alone with one escort. We would not reach the dock until the late morning, but excitement was rife among the passengers, many who had not set foot out of their home town, let alone England before joining the RAF, the next adventure was to begin on the morrow.

The ship docked during the night, and after breakfast the orders for disembarkation came over the Tannoy thick and fast. On the call for the Mess deck I was on, we picked our way through the still crowded ship to the gang plank and were met by a welcoming committee of the Ladies Welfare organisations of Halifax, who, as we climbed aboard the waiting train, gave out apples and other fruit, cold drinks, lemonade like you never tasted before, Coca Cola of course, and hot coffee. All on the house. A very fine gesture, by such lovely ladies who might in all probability never see any one of us again. The train left in the next hour, we were on our way to Moncton in New Brunswick to No. 31

Personnel Depot. Strange that all military units in Canada were called Depots.

We were to wait here for a posting to an E.F.T.S. The people of Moncton were very generous with their hospitality, they would gather together after church service a few of the lads, and take them home for Sunday dinner, then drive them back to the camp in the evenings. Many friendships were made and many a letter sent home to Britain giving news of sons in Canada.

By now it was August and parties of cadets would go to the beach at Shediac, and Pont du Chene on the St. Lawrence river, to enjoy a way of life the like of which we had not seen before. Swimming parties in the sea, baseball on the beach, cafes with hot-dogs, all those things we take for granted today.

It was from here that the Pan-Am Atlantic Clipper flying boats set off for Europe. We enjoyed those trips on the buses, to the beach, but were itching to get on to start our flying, waiting was a bore and the service was expert at arranging boredom. At every morning roll call we waited for our names and numbers to be called out and at the dismissal order for that day we were disappointed once more when WE were not called.

I stayed in the air crew depot at Moncton until the twelfth of August, when with several hundred potential Aircrew, I started a long train journey first to Montreal, where we were allowed a day in the town between trains, to see some of the sights, take some photographs, then it was back to another train, for a two day ride to Neepawa in Manitoba. The journey took us through the eastern stretches of Ontario on through to the forest lands of the north past Thunder Bay, Kenora and the masses of lakes and on into Manitoba and Winnipeg. The experiences on that train were most impressionable on the emotions of these young men, some almost fresh out of school, who had perhaps only travelled as far as the coast back home, on holiday trips, in those old Victorian era railway coaches of the LMS and GWR, without corridors or toilets.

The Canadian National Railway was a revelation, our coaches were attached to the regular TRANS-CANADIAN train leaving Montreal each day. The food served in the dining car, the fold down bunks for the night, the cloakrooms even, and the helpful attitude of the rail car attendants. We felt like royalty! At regular intervals we arrived at a stretch of double track, a passing loop, where we had to wait for the east bound train to pass, as the main line west was only single track, some of the waits could be as long as forty minutes or so. We were able to climb down on certain occasions, the fresh air was unbelievable, the fragrance of the pines around the track was heady. At Portage-la-Prairie, some way west of Winnipeg, our two coaches were detached and were taken on by another train to Neepawa, this would be our new training station for the next eight weeks.

No. 35 Elementary Flying Training School was run by a civilian company, with engineers supplied by the company and RAF personnel doing the flying instruction and administration. It was hot, with blue skies every day, perfect for flying and hopes were high that flying would soon begin. But first back to basics, the Canadian ground instructors forced us to repeat much of the theory we had done before in the UK, but now things were making so much more sense, since flying and ground tuition were happening on the same site and coincidental to each other, some days life dragged on tediously. On the flying side we made up for the boredom of classes, we flew every day, either morning or afternoon shift. Competition was fierce to attain several goals set by the trainees themselves, to reach high standards and obtain high pass marks was the dream of each one of us. Some of the aerobatics we attempted were difficult to perform, and some of the solo exercises were not according to the book, low flying was taboo in the training schools unless accompanied by an instructor. Ignore this order at your peril since culprits caught out were washed out immediately. Spinning in an aircraft was not a safe manoeuvre, but sheer bravado, was pushing some pupils too far, and ignoring safety rules was punishable, and inevitably we had 'Washouts.' The fifty cadets we began the course with was now dwindling, the flying programme was not easy, demanding full attention to all rules and recognition of serious or even dangerous attitudes of the aeroplane and how to take corrective action. Practise and more practice, was the order of the day. The Tiger Moths we were using differed from the original in so much that the Canadian versions were fitted with cockpit canopies, tail wheels and hand brakes. I liked them, enjoyed flying them, and as so often is said about this aeroplane, found them very forgiving.

Socially there was not much to the town, in home terms it would be called a village, the ice-cream parlour was very popular, the only bars where you could hope for a drink were to be found in the hotels. The buildings were 'clap-board' as seen in western movies. I think the only brick building was the bank, even the couple of churches were timber. On camp was a Church Army club, the Canadian equivalent to the Salvation Army for food and occasional entertainment, sometimes showing films, but high summer and the weather meant flying into late evening, plus a limited amount of night flying. One of the most striking sights, familiar to many these days, was the fantastic sight of the lights of Winnipeg from the air. My instructor had left the circuit, to fly towards the east, maybe for a half hour just to give me the chance to see this magnificent sight of such a large city at night. I finally soloed after three and a half hours dual, I then made two thirty minute flights solo. The Flight Commander's test was an important milestone; Pass and you went on, Fail and 'Curtains,' then a change in trade, maybe to become Bomb aimer or air gunner. My log book shows that I flew sixty-two hours total at Neepawa and was Rated as AVERAGE. Good! now to S.F.T.S. I wonder which, and where. It was at this time that I had to say goodbye to Jim Standen, my pal, over the past year, going right back to when we first joined at Lord's Cricket ground in London. He had been chosen to go to a school for twin engined training. I never saw him again. Which, turned out to be 41 S.F.T.S. (Service Flying Training School), and where, was Weyburn, Saskatchewan, about eighty miles south east of Regina the capital of the province. Here, I would fly the Harvard single engined trainer we had all hoped to train on, to some it seemed that 'Fighters' might be our future. This was not to be as you will learn.

We were nearing the Spanish coast so Dennis had come up alongside me for a better view, 'Should see Finisterre lighthouse in the next few minutes, Charlie,' he said. We were at least thirty miles away, but somewhere on the port beam the sweeping light should appear.

Across the bay the weather remained fine. Frank had kept radio silence but between obtaining bearings for Dennis, he also got the B.B.C. programme for the Forces, this livened things up until it went off air about midnight, we had coffee from the flasks, and sandwiches which the Mess at Melton had provided.

We had one alarm when I sensed something ahead, nothing obvious. Then I saw it, a dark shape in the gloom growing larger at an astonishing rate with two round glowing eyes, it was the glow of two exhaust rings and the flames from the exhaust pipes, gliding silently by on my starboard side at about two o-clock high. Friend or foe, we'll never find out. Not near enough to panic, but a shock at first, before realising that there was traffic moving in the opposite direction. It could have been one of the 511 Squadron Albemarles on the Azores route, of which I was to learn later.

'There's the light,' said Dennis 'Difficult to estimate how far away it is, still if we turn to a heading of 185 degrees we can parallel the coast.' The time was around two-thirty a.m. the rotating light swept across the sea at regular intervals we assumed it to be Finisterre, we had not received a briefing as to the code used. Strung like a gleaming necklace of pearls, the Spanish lights stretched to the horizon, for ever like a flare path beckoning us to the south. Further ahead we would reach

Portugal's lighted coast line to take us further on our way to the south, if the weather stayed fair they would guide us into the dawn. Tiredness was making itself felt. Frank was receiving signals from Gibraltar, but could not obtain accurate bearings, and since all messages were to be encoded, there was no point in communicating just for the sake of it. With so little to do it wasn't surprising that at this time in the flight he started to doze off.

The lights reminded me of the night near Winnipeg, and night flying at Weyburn when if we went on a cross country flight, to the north I could see Regina glowing like a ball of fire in the snow. Oh yes it snowed, our group was 'D' Flight, No. 1 Squadron. During October and early November life was hectic with class work taking many hours, yet flying had to continue. Some time in November it snowed for three days solid we were not able to fly until the runways were cleared, the snow ploughs began work as soon as the snow stopped falling, the snow was piled high along the side of the runways, and the approaches to them were cleared back for maybe two hundred yards, after the clearance work was completed it was back into the air once more. We now understood the reason for the rubber over boots we had been issued with, for our feet would have been soaked in minutes, so each time we went to town it was on with the boots then, when indoors say at a dance, we had dry feet or shoes I should say.

I see that in my log book, that we went on cross country navigation exercises in Ansons, putting into practise the work learned in classes, place names like Assiniboia, Melville, Lampman, Pipe Stone Lake, Bulyea, Moose Jaw, Bienfait, all figure as turning points at some time or other. Some of these cross countries, were flown solo in the Harvard, many stories are told of losing a pencil, or map, or even the navigation computer, by dropping it into the bottom of the aeroplane. There was no floor just two plates, shoe width, to slide one's heels on when using rudder. For small objects, the trick was to roll the aeroplane inverted and hope the offending object would fall into the canopy, there to recover it. You only dropped things once usually. Bigger items were not only a danger, getting caught up in essential controls, but needing the airframe mechanic to open up the aeroplane to recover them.

The very low temperatures that followed the snow, caused the river in town to ice over several feet thick and the thought of learning to skate on ice, was a temptation we could not resist. Each of us raided our savings to buy a set of skates. A sports shop in town supplied them, and on to the ice we went to join what seemed like all the people of the town. Of course we were hopeless without proper instruction. At the camp the maintenance crews had boarded off an area the size of a small football pitch, they flooded this with several layers of water over the next few days, and lo and behold they had created an ice rink, we spent much of our spare time skating with the experienced skaters, teaching the novices. Great stuff.

By Christmas I had amassed eighty four hours flying, dual, solo, day and night in total on this camp. I flew twice on Christmas Eve both, formation and also instrument flying, then two days off! Christmas Day, when the officers served the meal in the airmen's mess at lunch time. They had theirs later in the Officer's Mess.

Then Boxing Day when, I joined three others to visit the home of a Scottish family, who had requested that several trainees should have a traditional Christmas in their home. This was typical of the hospitality of the Canadian people.

We had our moments in the air, one epic event, was when Ken Nichols coming back from a Cross-Country, at low level with his instructor, with two feet of the top of a telegraph pole, embedded in the leading edge of the port wing. The enquiry decided, that after a medical and eye testing, that poor old Ken would need corrective lenses fitted to his goggles. I met him years later in Morocco, he'd just brought a photo-recce Spitfire in from Benson, 'over the top' to Gib. via France and Spain then down to Rabat.

Rabat, we were off the Portuguese coast about thirty miles off shore. Lisbon had gone by as a large glow, smaller towns shone like tiny beacons, I was bleary eyed, the constant drone of the engines was almost hypnotic, I shook myself, then peered round the door into the navigator's position. It had been too quiet, it seemed like hours since anyone had spoken on the inter-com. Too true, there behind me was the reason, they were both slumped over their tables. Frank I spotted through the gap at the door hinge. It was four o'clock on my watch, on the thirteenth of March 1944, I was the only bloke awake. I could have gone to sleep myself given the chance. However, I opened the clear view screen on the upper left of the windscreen, there was a sudden rush of air from the inside of the aeroplane, like a vacuum cleaner in motion all of the foul air was sucked out, this was a better method of changing the air than opening the side windows. The noise of the engines wasn't as great and it was better for viewing. Soon it would be getting lighter, the sky was already turning a rosier colour on the horizon, and the land based lights dimming.

I must check the fuel tanks again, getting low, I checked the airspeed and height, the aeroplane had gained five hundred feet and the speed was up to one hundred and forty five knots. I adjusted the power to stop the climb, and trimmed the nose down to give a shallow descent to three thousand feet, this would reduce the fuel needs a little further. But starboard main, was the first of the tanks to show empty on the gauges.

Around five-thirty, the dawn was definitely near. Over the arch of the sky the colours changed from orange, in the east, through the greens, to blue, and indigo, and finally, to the west where it was still black. I felt a tap on my elbow it was Dennis.

Feeling better now?' I asked.

'Yes' he replied 'why did you let me sleep?'

'I thought, that if I needed you, I could give you a shout. Is Frank awake?'

'Yes down the back end on the loo. He'll be back soon to get me some bearings from Gibraltar and Rabat, then I can work out a good fix of our position.'

'How is the fuel state'

'Very low, I'll need soon to go to the nacelle tanks' I had decided on my plan I would wait for the first signs of fuel starvation on whichever engine, select nacelle tank and cross feed at the same time, ensure smooth running, turn off main tank that side, then the crossfeed hopefully only one engine would cut out at a time.

Dennis had received the bearings from Frank, and gave me a new course to steer. I set the compass and made the turn southeasterly, the sun now coming round to shine through the forward windscreen, the sea below was a brilliant blue, not a cloud in the sky. I change the fuel cocks, without waiting for troubles, all the tank gauges were reading empty, we had one hundred and fourteen gallons in the nacelle tanks, and that represented roughly two hours flying time. Now all three of us were in the front cockpit peering ahead through the sun's glare for signs of the coast of Africa the so called Dark Continent. I don't remember who saw it first, it did not matter who, since as we got nearer, the brilliance of the sky was edged with an equally brilliant green at the coast line behind the white of the breaking waves.

We had passed the seven hour mark, things would not be tight after all, I called the Tower on V.H.F. notifying them that we were approaching, they acknowledged and gave me a course correction, to steer. Within thirty minutes I was over the airfield.

Not a bit like England or Canada, the runway was a strange green and sandy brown colour, the moment I put the aeroplane down on it I got a surprise, we rattled along with wisps of sand blown up by the propellers, it was a metal grid runway laid down by American Sea-Bees at the time of the North African landings. The steel grid bound the sand together allowing the sparse grass to bind together and hold. I followed the jeep that came out to the end of the runway to lead us to the dispersal. We had arrived in Rabat! Seven hours and forty five minutes from Hurn.

This was not the end, however we had first to remove all the loose equipment which was part of the aircraft inventory, load this with our personal kit, on to a truck, then go to the equipment stores to check in the flasks, navigation gear, torches watches, etc. and sign off our obligations. Of course, something had disappeared, and was unaccounted for, Dennis wasn't able to find a set of dividers, in the nav's kit. They probably, had fallen behind the navigator's desk and were now in the bowels of the fuselage, we had to pay up! Next an airman arrives from the dispersal with further bad news; Frank had committed the unforgivable sin, for wireless operators! He'd forgotten to wind in the trailing aerial before landing, the weighted end had caught on the metal runway grid, the aerial had been torn off. Another whip round putting the cash in the hat again to pay. At this rate we would not be able to afford the cost of delivering any more aeroplanes this month!

Hunger, and above all tiredness, were our problems, we were driven down to the transit billets given a bed each, and directed to the Sgt's Mess, where breakfast was being served. A free day had been granted, anyway we should be allowed at least eight hours off duty, after the night flight. Lying on the bed, it wasn't long before I fell into a deep sleep. The next memory, is the warmth of the afternoon, when I awoke, the others had already risen, and had found details of where to go to town, where to find the paymaster to get Francs, and what time the truck left the camp. This sounds so formal now in the light of later experiences, but we were

'Sprogs' in a foreign land suffice to say we found the haunts. I recall the name of a bistro, Le COQ d'OR frequented by the local RAF lads, joining in with the usual ribald songs, sung throughout the world by British forces, plus the contemporary songs of film and radio. We did not see that much of Rabat, it would be remedied in the future when we got 'our knees brown,' a hackneyed expression of the day, for new arrivals to the sunnier climes.

CHAPTER THREE

Phase two, of our flight to join our new unit, began the following day March 14th 1944, at about four thirty in the morning, when we were awakened with orders to report to the Operations Room, in half an hour to be briefed on the trip to Cairo where we were due to report to 216 Group HQ. A quick wash and curses from Frank that he didn't have enough time to shave, he had the quickest growing beard of any one I knew and often shaved twice each day, once for the usual morning do and again if going out in the evening. Dennis and I convinced him that he looked fine, so with a quick bite for breakfast, we leapt into the jeep that had been sent for us. The Officer in charge of the Operations room would become a good friend in the months to come. He was responsible for allocating crews to the aircraft to be delivered, he gave me the number M.F.136 as the aeroplane we were to take forward to Cairo.

We went to the stores once more, but without Dennis, who had gone off to the Met. Office to gather weather information. Loading up the truck took a while, since several crews were due to leave at the same time, the ensuing scramble to get a place on the truck was a disorganised shambles. Once you got your kit onto the truck you tried to convince the driver to take off for the dispersal tent immediately, and almost like a butler at the Manor he tried to organise 'his gentlemen' into the order that suited him. However, as each truck was filled, he had no excuse and off he went like some madman trying to win a Grand Prix. At the dispersal tent we stopped for I had to check and sign the Form '700,' the report that was signed by each tradesman that he had completed his inspection, and made any necessary repairs. The 'Chiefy' the F/Sgt in charge of servicing and refuelling, signed overall, and I signed to signify my acceptance of the aeroplane. During training I was only required to sign for solo flights, now it was becoming part of my daily routine.

Off to the flight lines, where lines and lines of aeroplanes of all types stood waiting their ultimate destiny. I settled down to the loading and the necessary checks of the aeroplane, then with all aboard ready, and with all pre-flight checks done, I got clearance from the tower, and taxied to the end of the runway, where I went through the routine to ready the Wellington for take-off. With clearance obtained, I began the take-off roll facing to the West, and climbed away steadily and on reaching five hundred feet, I began a gentle turn on to course for Fez in the east.

As we climbed towards our safe height of five thousand feet, we entered cloud at about two thousand, this was the low coastal mist which forms every morning, only to be burned off within a few hours. It wasn't very thick, at four thousand the sun broke in a dazzling blaze, it was impossible to see without sunglasses, the 'issue' pattern were great for the job. I finally stopped the climb at seven thousand, a height enough to clear the earlier ranges of mountains before crossing into Algeria.

This fantastic sight of the rising Sun was to be the regular departure feature when leaving from Rabat. I have never forgotten the huge orb of the rising Sun, as it slowly breaks away from the horizon. The landscape below wasn't visible for quite some time. In this so very clear air it was as if we had arrived on a new planet. So clear we could see what seemed like hundreds of miles around us. Just like Canada last winter when, after Ground school examinations, and Chief Flying instructors test, we enjoyed a short spell, of maybe two weeks, when we were allowed to do general flying. Practising some of our weaker exercises but loving every minute of solo time in the air. The final day came the lists were published, we were called into the flight commander's office to receive our assessments.

'Passed OK.'

'GREAT.' Then the crunch question what of the Ground school results? Were they good enough to achieve an award of my Wings? Good passes throughout, were the results I had hoped for, high marks in Navigation and meteorology. But a disappointment to follow, no Commission. So Sergeant Matthews it would be, I wasn't alone on the flight, those who had qualified, were split almost evenly between Sergeant Pilots and Pilot Officers, we had a Wings parade at which I received my Pilot's Brevet from a Canadian Colonel of some local regiment. Didn't care which! I'd got my wings at last.

Forget your Fighter pilots, we were told. 'The Air Force needs Bomber pilots.' This was a catastrophe. Why had we done all this time on Harvards only to have to make a change to twin-engined aircraft, and take the course to convert to them, putting us further back in the line for our return to the UK.

A gateway was to open however, there were various needs in other Commands. If one's grades were high enough, we were allowed to volunteer for Flying instructor training, or Coastal command. There were vacancies on a General Reconnaissance course, I volunteered, maybe, my excuse, to stay with a few other mates, so finally we left Weyburn for the long train ride to Prince Edward Island, in the St. Lawrence River.

On February 20 several of the new intake arrived in Charlottetown Prince Edward Island, to be informed that owing to bad weather, it would not be possible to start the next course on time. Two days later we were all moved to the nearby unit at Summerside where they immediately sent half of us on a week's leave. To cross the stretch of water between the mainland and the island, a ferry was used, and on our return from leave the ice on the river was several feet thick. The ferry boat made heavy work of breaking through to create a passage, when within a couple of miles of the destination bank we came to a complete halt, the captain said 'he could go no further' then proceeded to reverse along the channel he had broken. This sort of shunting to and fro, continued for some five hours until we eventually got to our destination, very cold and tired.

I spent my leave in St. John, New Brunswick. It was less cold here, but there was quite a bit of snow outside town. In the foyer of the Capitol Theatre, was the City Hospitality Centre, whose Secretary tried to place Service men with her volunteer Family hosts. I tried out the system, and was given instructions on how to find the home of a family, who would look after me for a few days. They were kind and considerate to a stranger who was far from home, but winter in Canada means staying indoors, this can be boring to young people, so I made my excuses and returned to the hostel I was booked in and rejoined my pals. In town we could visit cinemas and dance halls, have a drink in good company and generally have a good time. When the leave was over, on returning to Summerside the thaw had begun and the crossing to the island went off without a hitch.

  A G.R. course requires one to learn subjects such as Ship recognition, especially war ships, of the combatant nations, Germany, Italy, Japan, America, Russia. Signalling both by wireless and Aldis lamp. We studied further Navigation relevant to Coastal Command including the patterns adopted for sea searches, whether for surface vessels or submarines. The special coding systems for use between aircraft and naval ships when using radio or flares, Very Lights. All of the ground school work was paralleled with airborne exercises in the faithful old Anson, the work horses of Training Command. We flew night photo recces, over the ports on the St. Lawrence river, such as Chatham and Bathurst, and during day exercises flew simulated photographic runs over industrial sites in the coastal towns. On some of the low level flights over the New Brunswick countryside on the mainland we must have been really low to judge from some of the photographs of local farm buildings, I have in my books. I swear you could almost look into the windows and see the occupants, how they put up with the staff pilots flying so low I do not know. I flew a total of thirty seven hours, in those cold and draughty Ansons. Why did the trainees get the job of hand winding the undercarriage up or down? Each of the pilots and navigators helped one another doing our out of class studying, we were determined to succeed. And the end of April, early May finally arrived with the news of our success and the postings. I was to report to 31 Operational Training Unit at Debert, Nova Scotia, once again missing out on the boat that takes us home. Ah well Canada isn't that bad anyway.

Not wanting to travel by ferry again, eight of us bought a ticket to fly to Moncton on the mainland, it cost about ten dollars, three pounds, each and saved almost a day compared with the boat, and train, and I had friends in Moncton to visit. The aeroplane was a Lockheed Electra, in which I would enjoy flying in the next few weeks. The R.A.F. called it the Hudson.

31 O.T.U. Debert, was on the northern bank of the Bay of Fundy, a few miles from Truro, in a sandy scrubby area, very flat and as an airfield it had its problems. There is a tidal bore, similar to the river Severn over here in England, and when this is coming in, giving the right conditions, the fog comes following in at high speed. The airfield could become totally Blind in minutes, then if you were not down, you had no choice but to divert. There were two other fields on the opposite bank, and often there were short stop overs away from base. I converted to the Hudson and flew solo after twelve hours dual, in the day mode. This I reckon to be quite an achievement, since the change from a single engined Harvard, was something of a stride rather than a step. Then it took two hours twenty minutes, to solo at night. At this time I had been joined by my crew of Sgt's, Dennis Cooke, navigator, Frank Allaire and Bruce Dickie both wireless operator/air gunners, they would come on every trip possible, even if they were not required to be there, just for the air experience. We

changed to No. 2 Squadron where we got down to the serious business, of extending our crew activities, Air to Air Gunnery, bombing on the range, radio assisted blind approaches, where you have to have a blind faith in the operator in the Radio hut. We made dummy depth charge attacks on a Royal Canadian Navy submarine, which we had to find in the Bay and carry out a dummy run with smoke bombs, the Captain joined in, jovially offering a bottle of grog if a hit was scored, many evenings were spent by our course tippling at his expense, after our successes on the target. The last fourteen days here, were spent doing sea searches for enemy submarines operating off the coast near Halifax, the German U-boats were active on that side of the Atlantic also, these trips lasted around three hours. On one search when about a hundred miles off Halifax, in very misty weather, at around a thousand feet altitude, we were confronted by a US Navy Hellcat which was warning us off the route we were taking. Below was a major aircraft carrier, the Ranger on a routine exercise and we were in their air space, we had not received a briefing that the fleet would be in the area, but knowing the trigger happy gunners on board ship, we left the site with haste. On another patrol a friend, who had come through the courses with me to Debert, attacked a submarine on the surface about to dive, my friend did all the right things and returned to the location after half an hour and found some wreckage, his observer had made some great photos of the strike. Later it was confirmed that indeed, he had sunk the U-boat, the Canadian navy having found the boat on the bottom. For this action, my friend Sgt. Wallace was awarded the DFM on his OTU course.

A special search was called, on another occasion, when one of our trainee crews went missing, believed down, somewhere, in the St Lawrence estuary. We put up seven aircraft, to search for them but after several hours flying until dusk, found nothing. The Royal Canadian Navy took over the search but also were unable to discover any signs of the crew. I left Debert August 10th, and, at the invitation of Frank spent my leave on a visit with his family in Montreal.

CHAPTER FOUR

Fez duly came up and it was time to change course for Biskra. I turned more to the east, compass course 105 degrees magnetic roughly, the Atlas Mountains were both below and ahead. I increased the power to make the climb to ten thousand feet, and listened to the radio programme, Frank had put onto the intercom. Vera Lynn I expect and those flaming 'White Cliffs of Dover.'

Three hours to go, firstly over the Moroccan Atlas peaks then into Algeria for the next leg, we over flew Oujda which was to become our future base and headed out over the Saharan Atlas mountains interesting, but not spectacular. Now our course was more north-easterly, in the north the High Atlas highlighted by the bright sun, to the south through the glare of the sun, faintly visible, the sands of the Sahara and the rest of Africa. The four hundred miles across Algeria took about three hours and with thirty minutes to go, I called Biskra, on the VHF, no radio silence here, the enemy was almost a thousand miles away in central Italy. At my request, Biskra D.F. unit, gave a course to steer, to home-in on the aerodrome, a little later the aerodrome came into sight, WELL! our first experience of a desert strip, rolled sand stripped of all rocks and rubble then wetted twice per week, and with a central line marking the central landing line of the runway, this was made by pouring old engine oil from a drum carried on the back of a truck. On arrival we chased after the jeep with the Follow Me sign on the back, to the parking site for the aircraft near the flight tent. I booked in to the ground crew and reported the aircraft status, then requested full tanks for the next day, only then could we board the jeep to go to the transit Mess.

The track led through lines of date palms, past a cemetery, an eerie place, with strange ornate tombs on the surface of the ground, each with its vent to allow the 'Spirit' to ascend to Heaven, some of the poorer graves were only heaps of stones covering the coffins, the smell was not what one would expect. The road went on toward the town of Biskra, which in those days was the terminus of the railway from the north, it seemed little more than an oasis when looked on from the air. Turning into a drive through more palms, we arrived at the main doors of a huge stone built hotel, set among orange bushes and palms, flower beds and lawns. It was beautiful, but to these three weary travellers it glory would have to wait.

Inside, the walls and floors were marble, decorated columns supported the upper floors, the RAF personnel had done their best to make things comfortable, but it was an incongruous sight, to see 'issue' camp beds lining the walls of such opulent rooms, complete with their mosquito nets above. Washed, changed, rested, and fed, we made for the bar. Here to slake our thirst and remain in the cool; outside at five in the afternoon the temperature was still in the seventies/eighties.

Biskra was a Staging post on the route to the east, these posts were sited at convenient points along the routes to the East and Far East. They were used by Ferry crews as well as regular transports. Several flights could need to night stop so it required that there would be enough accommodation, the RAF supplied the administrative staff and employed either the local people to do cleaning and general duties, or in some cases prisoners of war, mostly Italian. They were very friendly places especially in the bar where you might, if not careful, have a round of ten or more, to buy drinks for if things got too friendly. This night turned out to be one such special occasion, propping up the bar was a civilian, a bit rotund, with a jolly red-cheeked face, who was telling ribald stories in a loud voice, he was Nosmo King a comedian, of the pre-war Music hall circuits. He gagged, we laughed, right through till the small hours.

Biskra to Castel Benito was three hours flying time, the procedures were the same for every flight, check in, sign the 700, etc. not to be dwelt on hereafter. After an uneventful run across the border into Tunisia, over the salt lakes, almost dried up now, as the spring weather hotted things up, flying south east over featureless sepia coloured land, across another border into Libya, not Ghaddafi's, but the ex. colony of Mussolini hence the name, Castel Benito, the airport for the capital, Tripoli. The airfield was littered with wrecked Italian, German, and some British aeroplanes, mostly fighters, this was my first chance to browse over enemy planes, in fact they were some of the first I had ever seen. The sight of these defeated aeroplanes made me feel sad, I enjoyed flying so much that these birds with their broken wings, were not to be gloated over. Their magnificence was gone now, they were useless. I turned away and headed for the Transit Mess to seek a meal and a bed.

The Mess was a small marquee-style tent with the walls rolled up to give more air, better than nothing, the food was OK, our mess kit was at the bottom of our kit bags in the aeroplane on the airfield, so we were scrounging tin plates and mugs off the mess staff. When asking for a bed they showed us to a tent with steel beds with the mesh top bare, no mattresses, no blankets, no nothing. It wasn't a Staging post and therefore was not equipped to cater to the needs of such iterants as us, we made the best of it, and decided on a hurried exit the next morning.

The mornings were always bright and sunny with blue skies these days, I guess that we were enjoying every minute of these new experiences. We did not fly across the Gulf of Sirte, but paralleled the coast ever more to the south east, until near El Agheilla, a change of course took us on to a north of east heading, on the leg into Egypt. The briefing for this leg was to maintain a track closer to the coast since in the case of having to put the aeroplane down, it would be close to the Desert road from where rescue would be easier. The desert wasn't all sand and dunes here, more of a scrub with patches of grass and bits of bush, the one thing that was most prominent was the pattern of tank tracks remaining from the battles over these many miles of desert. Derelict vehicles were everywhere and rusty equipment of all sorts friend and foe presumably, awaiting rescue still or maybe not. To see this amount of detail it must be plain that I was flying lower on this stretch of the journey, perhaps as low as about one thousand feet.

Near El Alamein there is the first of the Military Cemeteries, as we passed over it was still in the course of construction. To see so many tombstones! it only made one wonder if it was all worth while.

Cairo West the main airfield, lies beside the desert road between Giza site of the pyramids and Alexandria, when we arrived we found long tarmac runways, a few administration buildings, and messes, but no accommodation blocks, tents again, temporary we were told. When you entered the tent you went down several steps to find the ridge tents had been erected over an oblong stone and concrete box. Inside were four camp beds and small lockers, nice and cosy. Cool, during the day, warm at night. Only one night did we stay, since on the morrow it was into the city and Heliopolis to report to 216 Group who would decide to which unit we would be posted.

At Heliopolis, Group set us up with pay, Ferry Crew Priority Passes, and said we were to report to the Air Booking Office in the city to take the overnight flight to Oujda. No. 3 Aircraft Delivery Unit, Oujda, Morocco. All the way back across Northern Africa almost to Rabat! Some posting, some well considered decision making, who are we to argue? That night around eleven o'clock the gharry, I'm getting into the swing of things now, the Gypo name we used for any transport, truck, jeep, fifteen hundredweight etc, drove the passengers out to Cairo West there to join the crew of a Dakota of a Middle East transport squadron, which plied the route much like the airlines of today. For the record, the Dakota was FL 553 flown by F/o Rivalant, I believe of 216 Squadron, this squadron was the resident transport unit of the Middle East having been formed in the delta area of Egypt, during the First World War and based mostly at Heliopolis. The trip to Oujda took two days, Cairo, to Castel Benito, via Marble Arch, on 20th of March and then to Oujda via Biskra the next day.

Our new home at last! Here to report in, find our way round, go to the Sergeants Mess, sign in, find a bed space and do all those myriad things a new arrival has to do. The airfield had one runway it was sand with steel planking, the barracks were French Armee de l'air buildings and very comfortable. The Mess had a bar and facilities where to buy NAAFI goods, and a laundry service, who ran it I never knew, but it was a godsend to the flying crews who spent so little time at base. In a room on the other side of the square, the availability board showed the location of all air crew. Metal discs with one's name punch in, were hung in crew order, either as 'on route', 'at base', 'on leave'.

A section was reserved for notifying crews of their next duty turn. The tags were hung in vertical rows with Skipper at the top then Nav. and WOP. below. At a glance it was possible to check who was available, and who would be off in the morning on the first flight to Rabat, or in the case of those who ferried fighters. Singles, we called them, who would go to Casablanca, where their aircraft were assembled.

One day off, then the work started in earnest, --- away to Rabat, the first delivery a Wellington Mark X111 to Blida near Algiers, take a truck to Maison Blanche, the airfield for Algiers, Dakota to Oujda. That short sentence tells the essentials only, of two days, three flights, one truck ride, and a distance flown of fifteen hundred miles. This was to be our way of life for the foreseeable future. That was up to March 26th, by the end of March we were in Cairo again having taken through a Wellington X, but we had three or four days to sample the delights of Cairo, before returning to base. The return flights to Oujda, from Cairo could last as long as thirteen and a half hours, spread over two days. One didn't get far at only one hundred and forty five knots.

During the next month, May 1944, as we settled into the routine my crew and I delivered twelve aircraft to various Maintenance Units, or airfields. They included several marks of the Wellington, the oldest being a Mark 1c with Pegasus engines as per the original, kitted out as a passenger carrier with eight or ten seats in the rear fuselage. Also a couple of Warwicks these were the Air/Sea Rescue versions, one complete with its airborne lifeboat attached. On arrival back at base I had to admit to flying the Warwick without having had dual instruction on the type prior to any delivery of the aircraft.

The Squadron Leader signed me up, as authorised to fly them, with a reprimand, that in future, I request for a conversion. The hours flown were thirty nine and forty five minutes on delivery, with a further forty hours being flown back as passengers. Setif, in Algeria, Bari and Foggia in Italy, and Catania in Sicily, were our destinations. The work load was pretty high, we had easily reached our monthly maximum, flying on 25 days of the month. This has to be read in the context that flying in or through bad weather or at night was not permitted since the aircraft were almost brand new, and the squadrons up front needed them in good shape. We flew unarmed with only two or three crew, or when pilot navigated, just Frank and I, then more often than not we flew along the coast line.

The use of the different Sgt's Messes or Transit sites, over the area gave a catalogue of which could offer the best food, what day of the month cigarette rations were available, who poured the best pint, or which night there would be a dance in town or in the camp. So as the months went by we delivered our aeroplanes and planned our 'stop overs' with all those good things in mind. It was possible that having delivered to an MU. there could be something to move on, in these circumstances we did not get back to base for some weeks. Living out of a flight bag was no joke, it wasn't possible to get laundry done at many places down the route, unless you bribed some Arab servant in the Mess or maybe an Italian POW. It was surprising how much laundry it was possible to have done for a bar of soap, or five cigarettes.

CHAPTER FIVE

Referring back to training and Canada. The voyage back was on the RMS Queen Elizabeth, the original of that name. She had not seen passenger service since her launch in 1939, she was a troop ship first and last. I was separated from my crew and to my surprise, found that I no longer suffered from sea sickness. The trip across was without incident, the Canadian air cover stayed with us for a day and a half, we were sailing at near thirty knots zig zag pattern changing each thirty minutes. As soon as we were outside the limit of range of the aeroplanes, we had forebodings until Liberators from Iceland or N. Ireland took over about a day later. The ship ripped through the water at a high speed no zig zag pattern now straight as an arrow until the aircraft arrived. The first one in flew low over the water, that was a marvellous sight from where I was on an upper deck luckily on the correct side, Port I think, since he roared in on my left going from left to right, the co-pilot waving and all the guys on the ship waving back. A day later we had Spitfires coming in at regular intervals to cheer us up, the fact they were here, meant we were closer to Ireland or Scotland than we dare hope.

So on into the Clyde, I don't remember whether it was night or day, I didn't see land until I disembarked. Perhaps I was in one of those queues, which seemed to stretch all around the ship to get to the mess deck, with fifteen thousand troops on board life had been hectic. Still I had a kit bag full of nylon stockings, chocolate, cigarettes and make up, perfume etc. for my wife. Boarding a train on the dockside at Gourock I journeyed to Harrogate, where many, many air crew were waiting for posting to squadrons. The accommodation was in the large hotels commandeered for the purpose, mine was the Majestic or Imperial or whatever, only Pilots here, Navigators at some other site. Frank with, the rest of the Canadians were sent to Bournemouth in Dorset. First priority, was a spell of leave both by entitlement, and the need to reduce the number of 'bods' in the unit.

I went home to see my beautiful, new daughter, who had been born the previous August, during my course at Neepawa. The chocolate came in handy to break the ice, between father and daughter. She had been christened Dorothy and had difficulty accepting this new person in mummy's life. The whole family made merry for those several days, relatives suddenly became closer, on seeing the cartons of American cigarettes, and the nylons, chocolates, and other goodies coming out of my kit bags. I visited my mum, saw my brother, who had nicked my bike and then swapped it, I did the rounds, then it was all over. My only trip home gone in a few days.

At Harrogate they had problems! Too many air crew with nothing to occupy them, a big mix of ranks F/sgts. W/os, as well as all those Sgt's, so many of the guys confined here had been instructors or 'Stooge' pilots over in Canada often between operational tours. Discipline was hard to maintain among these headstrong youths, for example a group of ten of us were sent to the Motor pool to work, not us! Either, scrounge a ride south on the first truck going that way, or as in my case, I opted to visit my wife's relatives in South Shields. She had uncles, aunts, and grandmothers there, whom I had yet to meet, since her immediate family had migrated to Coventry in 1940. 'To dodge the German attacks on the riverside industries' her Dad said in justifying the move.

I had an address for Grandma Smith, her dad's mother, who maybe would show me around. I didn't have a pass to be off camp, beyond the allowed twenty miles but who cared. I was a Sgt. Pilot of six months standing, and lucky for the time, still alive. I had a terrific time taken out to tea here, there and everywhere, this aunt, that aunt, so it went on. 'This is young Margaret's man from Coventry.' At night down to the pub where it was impossible to stand my round. All good things come to an end, I left to catch my train, fully approved of by my new relations, and a spring in my step.

At Newcastle station I got my 'come-uppance,' I was accosted by two Service Policemen, and could not talk my way out of this, so resigned myself to the indignity of admitting I was out of bounds without a pass. What a shame for those Corporals, as the Adjutant said, when I had to explain the incident, 'You can have a pass any time, you wish, provided you're here for first parade on a Monday' the day when posting lists were read out.

Eight weeks I wasted in Harrogate, until the day arrived when my name was on the roll, who made them up I still do not know, but by a remarkable piece of good fortune, you could not admit that it was planned, when, I arrived at 104 Transport OTU. Nutts Corner, outside Belfast on November 23rd. 1943 I was reunited with Frank and Dennis, no sign of Bruce. Just 25 months, more than two years, since first I trod the hallowed turf at Lord's Cricket, ground, ACRC, here again I was on yet another course and with the prospect of changing to another type to learn to fly. The weather was generally foul, rain most days, bitterly cold and raw winds, I reckoned even the birds had stopped flying. We had classes each day re-doing many of the things previously studied, and did not get into the flying programme until New Year's Day.

Yet another Christmas was to be spent away from home, I was getting used with it, most of us were now succumbing to late nights in the bar and thick heads in the mornings. By the end of January the flying was completed, and we got a shock when a medical parade was called for us to receive our batch of 'jabs' for overseas duties. Not only the usual tetanus, and TAB. but also Yellow Fever and Smallpox vaccination to cap it all. The way round the agony of the side effects was to go into Belfast and down a few pints of Guinness.

During the conversion to Wellingtons, mark fours in this case with American Twin Wasp engines, I went solo after four hours dual instruction, which wasn't without a hitch. For some reason I had great difficulty with the aeroplane wanting to swing off to the right on take-off, which was a normal tendency for this type but it was easy to over correct and develop, an even worse swing to the left which often ended in running off the runway into the mud and up to the wheel axles, in the first phase.

However I was to discover that the optimum method of starting the take-off run, was to lead with the right hand throttle and follow up with the left to keep the aeroplane straight, then as one gained rudder effectiveness the throttles could be run up to full power synchronously. This conversion to a new type was at a satellite airfield called Mullaghmore to the north of our base and near to Coleraine and Ballymoney, the best day in town in Coleraine was market day when the pubs were open all day. The next two weeks were occupied with Navigational exercises, both by day and night, the weather was appalling, even the birds were still grounded.

    Day flights were not so bad, we flew to South Wales then up to Shawbury, in Shropshire on one occasion, where I got confused with which airfield I had arrived at, the tower signals had approved the landing, and given the runway in use and airfield pressure to set the altimeter. When I landed and dropped off my three passengers, I remarked on the shortness of the runway, to the duty operations officer in the tower, and discovered I had landed at a fighter training unit, a satellite of Ternhill nearby, the longest runway they had was only 1100 yds with a railway line on a low embankment and its telephone wires, at the end of the runway. I elected to use it whatever the outcome, I felt sure the Wimpy would be able to clear all obstacles facing us. It was a hairy take-off, I used about fifteen degrees of flap, as much throttle as I could control, with the brakes held on, then faced the prospect of the dreaded swing to the left when I loosened the brakes. We roared away. I forced the tail into the air pushing hard forwards on the control column, with the tail high in the air, I waited for the rudder to begin to react to the air flow, the aeroplane gathered speed, not fast enough for me, but we were committed I maintain the forward pressure on the stick, as long as I dared, noted the air speed at one hundred knots and hauled the damned thing into the air, we cleared the wires so I could ease forward a little to let the airspeed rise and the aeroplane climb away. Not often did we have the problem of short runways.

The number of nav. exercises at the Transport OTU. had been reduced, by the Chief Instructor in view of the number we had carried out at Debert, earlier that year. We had done a full complement at our previous OTU, albeit that it was at least six months ago. The first night nav. was in the most atrocious weather, a four hundred miles flight out over the Atlantic with a Staff crew on board to assess us. It was raining like the clappers on take-off, with a wind speed at ground level of more than forty knots, and the cloud base at only two thousand feet. Climbing out after a dicey take-off I turned to the north for the coast of Ireland near Portrush, the few lights on the aerodrome soon disappeared, as we entered the cloud, it would be flying on instruments from here onward, maybe all night.

I followed Dennis's courses, straining to fly on manual since the auto-pilot could not cope with the violent rolling and yawing of the aeroplane, the Staff pilot was on hand to assist. Dennis was reporting calculated wind speeds in excess of ninety miles per hour. It would be impossible to reach our intended turning point and have enough fuel to get back to Nutts Corner. The staff members decided that we should turn at the estimated time we were due to reach the calculated position. For three hours we flew blind out to the west over the Atlantic ocean gathering ice all the time, on the wings, on the control surfaces, buffeted by the turbulence, blinded at times by the lightning flashes. A thoroughly disturbing experience, so much so that my two trusted crew became violently air sick and were out of action for the rest of the flight.

The Staff wireless operator, and navigator took over their duties. At the limit of this long leg out to the west we had a lightning strike on the aeroplane. This left the aircraft surrounded in a glow which they call St. Elmo's fire. A brilliant ball of purple was enveloping the whole aeroplane, everything was glowing like some gigantic glow-worm or moth in the light of a bonfire. Most especially the propellers, which created a 'whirling ring of fire' on either side of the aeroplane, it would switch off almost as quickly as it came, then reappear at the next strike. This seemed to go on for an age. We desperately needed to change height to rid the aeroplane of the ice, lower was the only option for a rise in temperature really, if I could get us below the cloud base surely the ice would break away or melt.

Down toward the ocean we flew, after the reverse turn to head east at last. Below us the cloud thinned, we broke clear at around fifteen hundred feet. Taking account of the calculated wind speeds, it would be foolish to remain at this altitude too long, we were approaching the coast at a much greater ground speed than we left it, if we overshot our planned turning point for the leg south to base we had to face the fact that the Scottish mountains were not so far ahead. The W/OP got a continuous stream of bearings, but uncertain of our exact position I climbed again to four thousand feet.

When it came the course change, from the Navigator was a shock, 'Steer 265 degrees.'

'What?' I cried 'That's west.'

I was turning as I spoke, the automatic reaction to a course change is to always 'Turn first, argue afterwards,' our position was clearly too far east of our base, we flew for at least fifty minutes on this course, before at my request, the tower began the instructions for a G.C.A. approach. This involved guidance from the ground operators who used radar screens to monitor our approach for height, direction and rate of descent. The instructions they gave were so good that we broke through the cloud base at fourteen hundred feet safely above the top of Divis mountain, to see the Drem lights circling the aerodrome already lit. However, the landing prospects were not good, the Control Tower said, that the wind although down the runway, had increased in speed since take-off and was now blowing at fifty to fifty five knots, with some gusts higher still. Clearly close to an impossibly dangerous situation.

The turbulence had not ceased, if anything it became more severe the nearer the ground we were. Rounding the circuit lights and with all checks complete I turned into the final approach, the Staff Pilot was giving all the assistance possible, I had decided not to use much flap and motored steadily in. As soon as the throttles were reduced, we seemed to hang in the air, like a glider, or a balloon, the aeroplane would not sit down on the ground and floated and floated, until there wasn't enough runway left. I called 'Overshoot' raised the undercarriage, and went round again, the next attempt was no better, finally the tower offered a diversion to Prestwick. We considered this as we made yet another attempt to land, we said 'one more go,' it was no use, even without flap, the aeroplane was still flying down to eighty knots, no motor worth talking about, and in great danger of a stall. At that height NOT FUNNY..

Diversion it would be, clean up the aeroplane for a climb on course for Prestwick, wheels up - cooling gills, half - mixture, auto rich - climb power engine settings. It was as if the first four or five hours had not taken place, almost a new flight. With a new course set, and radio contact with both Nutts Corner and Prestwick the next stage was less eventful, we had a great letdown through cloud and approached the Finals in dry and smoother conditions, the landing was fine and six weary air crew climbed down from the aeroplane. They had said it was a Transport OTU. we were at, more like an operational flight in deteriorating weather. Six hours my log book records, four and a half of them on instruments, and all manually flown. The next day we slept through, then fully refreshed, on day three flew the forty five minutes back to base. That disastrous night we had no aircraft successfully land at base, two disappeared completely never to be heard of again, three landed at Prestwick, two more force landed on beaches off Scotland on the islands, two others landed at Tiree. A bad night for us all.

Within two more days the course was over, but not until after the most horrendous 'Binge' in history. Ours was the last course on this airfield, it would change to other duties after we had gone, even the ground crews didn't know their fate. In situations like this the remaining funds in the Sergeants Mess accounts, would revert to the Air Ministry, who maintained these in a fund to initiate new Mess funds on new sites, give them a float in other words. The funds represented the profits achieved by the Mess committee, who naturally resented giving to others, so -- a 'Mess Dance and Booze up' was planned by the committee, we trainees were invited to join in, the drinks and food would be free. Judging by what I saw this had been weeks in preparation. All the WAAF personnel were expected to attend and also two trucks had been sent to Belfast to bring in those who had accepted the invitation, young ladies of course, no chance of a dance without the ladies. I had fallen in with a motley crowd of Canadians, Aussies, and Kiwi's not to mention Scots, Welsh and English, suffice to say we hit the bottle with a vengeance seldom seen in civvy street. Behind the bar were five or six huge wooden barrels of beer, Guinness, and cider, then ranged up on separate tables, overseen by Mess stewards, every sort of spirit you could imagine, the whisky ran out at about eleven o'clock, so we changed to gin. I don't recall dancing, it seemed a waste of good drinking time. I do remember, having to go through the swing doors to get to the bar -- Frankie bringing glasses filled with doubles or even trebles, my last memory of that night was putting on a greatcoat to go back to my billet. Nothing more, not a thing until I awoke, when a shrill voice wanted to know if thing were all right. They certainly were not! I was sitting half lying, on an armchair with my feet on another close to one of those solid fuel stoves we had in the Nissan type huts in the Mess Hall. In the next chair was my Canadian W/o, friend 'Moose,' apparently he had found me lying beside the road at the base of a telephone pole, I must have blundered into it in the dark, banged my head and passed out. He apparently had dragged me back to the mess being nearer. The WAAF cook offered fried eggs and tea, I was ravenous and could not believe the events of the night before. Later I had to wash, muddy and blood stained, I was filthy, since I had lain for some time in the rain, and the Irish red mud did not help matters.

But cleaned up and changed into my other suit, I could face the day and get signed off, to go home for a week's leave. Not before I had handed in the blue battle dress in exchange for khaki, and receiving khaki drill shirts and shorts, long knee length socks, all the regulation gear for Middle East Service. Now it became obvious where we were headed, the Mediterranean or the Far East, we would find out soon enough! Meanwhile the train and the Stranraer ferry awaited and the passage home to Coventry.

CHAPTER SIX

To go on leave, was the ever present something on one's mind. How we could waste those precious days, the working members of the families were unapproachable for most of the week, both 'guys and gals.' The war effort demanded maximum hours from everyone, long days often ten hours at the work place, leisure was grabbed in the main, for the few hours in the week when you could.

'Hello, home again, you're always on leave' seemed to be a standard welcome, even after a lapse of many months. So Sunday was the best day to meet the workers, inevitably at the local, plenty of beers before Sunday dinner at 2 o'clock. This time I brought Frankie home with me, he was given free rein to do as he pleased much as I had in Montreal with his family, we visited Stratford upon Avon, Kenilworth, Birmingham, the city cinemas, etc. Margaret's sister kept him company, and it was she who came to the railway station to see us off, when Margaret waved the both of us goodbye.

Melton Mowbray in Leicestershire, had an airfield built beside the Burton Lazars road, on the high ground south of the town, it was a good site, above the fog layer and free from problems with the weather. The unit based here was 304 Ferry Transit Unit where some ferry tasks were carried out. I brought up three Wellingtons from RAF Kemble including LP 145 which was to become 'our' aeroplane in so much that we flew her on wireless tests, fuel consumption tests, and an air test before leaving, with all our goods and chattels for Hurn. The best memory of Melton sergeants mess was the way we made toast on the tortoise stove in the middle of the dining room, we would slap rounds of bread on the outside of the stove where they stuck to the hot metal until toasted when they fell off, it was possible to do two rounds while waiting in the queue for the meal.

During our stay in Melton we visited the local hostelries, on one occasion at a dance I witnessed the ultimate tomfoolery - an American paratrooper leaping from the balcony in the Odd Fellows Hall, screaming 'Geronimo' as if leaping from the door of a C.47, of course he injured himself, be broke two legs. I expect he missed the D-Day landings, just a couple of months away, lucky maybe, foolish for sure, drunk definitely!

At Hurn there were Albemarles towing gliders in practices, getting ready for the invasion of France in June, now this was the first time I had seen these aircraft in service with the RAF, my last memory of the Albemarle was at the Baginton Works of Armstrong Whitworth, the makers of this aeroplane, for I worked there in the drawing office from mid 1940 up to me joining the RAF in October 1941. Part of my job was to design special rigs for testing various systems in the aircraft, such things as a hydraulic pump unit to connect up, outside power driven, to test the function of the flaps or the undercarriage. I also worked on similar rigs for the earlier Whitley aeroplane which we were building alongside the Albemarles. The name Whitley came from the name of the aerodrome where the aeroplane was designed and built before the Baginton plant was started. In fact the Chief Designer still maintained his office at Whitley, although Baginton had been up and running for some five years at this time. I normally cycled the five miles to work each day. On the morning after the Coventry Blitz I had to carry my bicycle over my shoulder and walk for two or three miles, we lost two draughtsmen in that Air raid.

Many a lunch time I would often be found walking the length of the apron fronting the hangers, hoping for a sight of S/Ldr Turner Hughes, the Test Pilot, or as occasionally happened a damaged, wounded, old war bird, would be brought back by the crews who had flown in them. Mostly in a dreadful state with huge pieces shot off, on one occasion with one rudder and half an elevator completely missing. It showed the strength of the airframe, and the skill of the air crews, who were so full of praise for the makers and their workers, naturally the fliers were given the V.I.P. treatment and made a tour of the production lines, perhaps these happenings inspired me further to become a pilot. As a boy on hot summer days I would ride out to Baginton to watch the aeroplanes. AWA Ensigns with four Armstrong Siddley Tiger engines were a favourite and the Whitleys being produced for the RAF. In 1938 my old dad would not give his consent for me to join the RAF as a cadet at sixteen years of age and I had to wait until I was older.

However, enough of that we're here at Hurn getting our aeroplane refuelled, being vaccinated against smallpox as a last minute non-scheduled item, receiving an up to date weather report and waiting for ten o'clock for the start of our adventure.

CHAPTER SEVEN

Some of the trials of the job are found in the notes attached to the records of the flights I made, a good example is June 1944. I had been detailed to take a Warwick BV 395 to Cairo, I was to make a detour via Maison Blanche with three passengers, who were to collect Mustangs from there, to fly on to Sicily. This leg was fine we dropped the passengers, checked in and retired for the night, next morning on the flight line were two airmen, hoping for a ride to Cairo. I agreed provided they had their CO's approval chitty. Yes they had, all standard procedure. Almost immediately after take off the oil temperature shot off the clock, I throttled back on that side opened the cowl gills and made a swift return to the airfield. I reported the fault to the ground crew who took a couple of hours to repair and check the engine. With the all clear given we set off again. With daylight in short supply I had planned to night stop at Biskra, landing there at dusk, and requesting an early start on next day. In the knowledge that the two airmen passengers were on leave, I was trying to make up time. That morning I was hit by another bombshell, I gained two more passengers who this time were bound for Castel Benito. Landing there without a hitch, I managed a quick turn round, and after leaving the two Officers, who I had brought in, I set course for Cairo. This time taking the more direct route over the Gulf of Sirte, we could maintain radio contact with many of the airfields around, when at two and a half hours into this leg that same engine started to play up again, with high temperature readings on the oil gauge and falling oil-pressure. With plenty of height to spare, I eased back on the throttles, then started to steadily descend while I called the airfield at Benina, outside Benghazi, for assistance. They helped with courses to steer, and got us down after a three hour run from Castel Benito. Over night they worked on the engine such that the next morning Dennis and I were able to do the necessary Air test and pass off the ground crew's work, all aboard and again with four passengers we left for Cairo, the passengers we gained were some of the crew who had worked at night to fix the bird they were flying in today. Great faith!!

Finally arriving in Cairo we had taken five days, seven separate flights, and twelve hours twenty five minutes in the air to deliver one aeroplane and eight passengers to the big city -- and -- two more days, with fifteen hours, and forty minutes flying time, on six legs to get back again to base. Taking into account the lost days in Cairo, the total elapsed time was nine days, this wasn't a one off either, the weather and the restrictions on night flying caused many an unnecessary delay.

Another example was a delivery of a Wellington Mk. 13 to Takoradi on the Gold coast in July, August of that year. Two aborted attempts on the 29th and 30th of July, to get into Agadir in Morocco, as a diversion caused by bad weather, as we were bound for Port Etienne on the most southerly tip of Western Morocco, were caused directly by the weather. The hot moist air over the coast triggered off serious thunder storms on the first day, and keeping to the safety rules, I decided to turn back, and the time spent was one and a half hours on the first day, and four hours on the second, totally wasted. The following day, trying to make a better showing, we were this time off Agadir, in rough weather and with bad visibility. Frankie felt he had grasp of the very basic radar of those days, fitted to this Wimpy, good for sea sweeps not for the task we demanded of it the weather was so poor with torrential rain we made a run for the air strip at Agadir. I let down to about two hundred feet following the course that the new navigator to our crew, Ted McKenzie always referred to as Mac. suggested, with Frankie trying to monitor our distance from the shore line in the hope that the gloom would disperse before we got to the coast and could make a visual landing.

Twice I called it off with less than a mile to go to the coast, plus or minus what error there was in the radar readings; at least, hoping no minuses to put the aeroplane too close to the coastal hills. Each time I pulled up on a safety route out of the bay at very low levels there's nil time for dithering with decisions. Finally we gave it best again, return to Rabat, total time today four hours or so, culminating in the ops. officer complaining of my lack of skill at instrument flying, two differing things -- being chair bound at Rabat, -- or being up there in the 'clagg' easy to criticise another to be doing the flying and decision making, we would try again two days later.

This time no problems to reach Port Etienne, all six and a half hours free from aggravation, the sun shone, the sea a vivid blue beneath, and the ever present coast line to keep us company all the way down to the south. We enjoyed a late lunch at the Mess tent, the ground crew performed the miracle of refuelling my aeroplane with five hundred or so gallons of petrol, using huge funnels, from a truck loaded with Jerry cans. Even in the late afternoon the temperature was in the nineties, those lads sweated it out, and when they had finished, Mac, Frankie and I invited them to a few beers at the NAAFI hut.

    A leisurely start was made the next day, with no Ops bloke to chase us off his airfield, I was heading for the planned stop at Dakar in Senegal. A good trip the sand well behind, now flying over forests and rivers, the land a rich sea of green, not good for a forced landing, but there was always the coast and a beach if we were in need. Radio contact with Dakar came up with a terse 'Do not land' reply to my request for landing instructions, and 'What fuel reserves do you have?' Several hours yet was my response, I was instructed to divert to Waterloo in Sierra Leone, the final clue as to the problem came when we were informed that there was a strict quarantine order in effect as Bubonic plague was rife in the area. We were off to the south again, on the skyline ahead was a gathering of high cumulus cloud looking ominous, with the sun behind it, I initiated a climb with the intention of going over the top. Frankie requested a weather report from YunDum, the nearest airfield, in the Gambia, it wasn't good, heavy rain thunder gusty winds. Just as the report was complete, I was faced with a large kite hawk, often referred to as a shyte hawk, dead ahead in line with the windscreen, no time to think, shove the control column forward, the bird went over the cockpit canopy, then thud, thud, thud toward the tail end. Bird strike! No immediate visible damage all controls working, next into the cloud massed ahead, tossing in the turbulence of the cumulonimbus cloud, flashes of lightning, thoroughly unpleasant, for was it not the 'rainy season,' when it might rain for days on end. Calling up YunDum, on VHF revealed the aerials were damaged, no replies. When checked from the Astro-hatch, cor! no aerials at all, even the radar ASV's bent all out of shape.

Descending to two thousand feet brought the aeroplane below the cloud base, so Mac came up front and between us we map read our way to the Gambia river, to Bathurst then arrived over YunDum. When asked if they were receiving our transmissions the tower replied with a green flare, using green for yes and red for no, I was able to get the clearance to land and find the direction to approach. On inspecting the damage to the aeroplane it revealed a very large dent in the fin leading edge some two feet tall by six inches in depth. The row of ASV aerials on the top surface of the fuselage, which were nicknamed 'Christmas Trees,' had been struck to greater or lesser degrees, from front to back of the aeroplane. The wire aerials had all gone, so our next problem was could the ground staff at YunDum fix it. Did they have any spares etc.? The upshot was a delay of five days while the tradesmen made, fixed and straightened parts to make our Wimpy airworthy again, the radio mechanics made and fitted new aerials for the various sets and ground tested them, we would need an air test to clear their work. Meanwhile we fliers had a holiday being feted by the Sgt's Mess and given the VIP treatment by the black boys who acted as servants they were in fact soldiers of the West African Rifles hardly boys really. They had a great sense of fun, always smiling and seemingly pleased to see us on their patch. We gave them money to buy pineapples and for around a shilling they brought back four or five, this was a new treat for me.

I didn't ever remember having fresh pineapple at home, the concept of fresh exotic fruit to be had so easily, was an exciting new experience, which stays in my memory to this day. We made air tests, giving rides to the ground staff, we had photographs taken by the station photographer, posed in front of poor MF. 582 the injured Wimpy, now recovered to its flying state if nothing else. But holidays were not part of the job, had there been another aeroplane on the field due for delivery we would have had to take that one on.

From YunDum, Waterloo was three hours flying time, it was a rainy day with bright sunny stretches between the tropical showers. When it rained it was torrential the wipers on the wind screen could hardly cope but at height it did not seem to matter. On arrival at Waterloo the runway shone in the bright sunshine, 'Wet' I thought, 'watch it,' the Tower's only comment was 'A little water on the ground.'

After an uneventful approach and landing the natural question 'Will we stop, or slide?' There was four to five inches of water on the runway spraying high into the air from the prop wash, without treads on the tyres of the aeroplane there was little or no grip, it was prudent not to use the brakes, but steer by use of engine power, the water acted as the brake, hopefully.

The remainder of the delivery passed off without incident, night stopping at Robertsfield, in Liberia, where we got our first sighting of B.29 Superfortress's, on their way to the Far East, having crossed the Atlantic from the Bahamas. Then the last leg to Takoradi, Ghana, there at the MU. where the crated fighters arrived for assembly during 1940 to 1943, we handed over the aeroplane at last!

One over night stop, and off north again in a BOAC Dakota for the twenty five hours journey to Rabat. How come BOAC? Well our ferry crew passes gave us priority over most other travellers, I've seen Captains, Majors, Wing Commanders, pulled off at the last minute to accommodate ferry crew, however it was not often that such drastic action was necessary. We more often than not booked in for a flight two days hence, unless there was a very urgent need to get back. It was there if we needed it. Life went quietly to and fro up and down the route into mid September, when on the 12th I was told by my CO. to report to 1330 Conversion unit, this time I was to be denied the delivery flight, but flew passenger to Cairo on a 216 Squadron Dakota. My destination was to Bilbeis an airfield in the Nile delta to the north east of Cairo.

CHAPTER EIGHT

I reported to the Chief Instructor's office, on September 16th, to hand in my orders, it was only here that I was told of the reason for my move. I was to convert to Marauders, the infamous B26. with the nickname 'The Widow Maker.' Twin engined tricycle undercarriage, heavy, fast especially on the approach maybe one hundred and twenty m.p.h. or more.

My instructor was introduced to me as F/Lt. Bland, we became friends, over the next few days. I had a couple of days to familiarise myself with the fuel and hydraulic systems also the ignition and emergency procedures, this we did Chris Bland and I, in a more adult manner than school style. We settled into a corner of the crew room to study and for me to appreciate the knowledge, until on the 19th we began the flying tuition part of the course.

As more experienced Pilots, we were expected to gain the familiarity with the aeroplane on 'solo' flights, this was done by being in the air with other pilots who were training. So the first hour and a half, might be dual instruction then a similar spell as co-pilot to someone else, in training and he would be safety or co-pilot to another. With three to four hours instruction I was sent off as first pilot for two hours practising circuits and landings. No more tuition just practice with the other trainees. This only occupied four days to accumulate four hours dual, four hours as both first and co-pilot, so a useful twelve hours in the air.

I will admit to some misgivings at times when certain aspects of the aeroplane's traits were being demonstrated by Chris Bland. For instance, one day he was demonstrating the ability of the aeroplane to continue flying on one engine, we had closed the throttle, feathered the prop and trimmed out the controls to keep the aeroplane straight and level, the book says, 'set the good engine' to such and such a pitch and prop revolutions and maintain 175 knots. There we were at about ten thousand feet left leg stuck out to keep straight, loads of left aileron sweating like mad, yes we're straight, yes to level as far as the wings are concerned, but we're going down at about fifteen hundred feet per minute, six minutes to the deck. Needless to say we soon packed that game in. It just would not keep it's height. 'Lethal,' I remarked. 'Afraid so,' said Chris. With ferry tanks loaded it could make life dangerous, at best it was a controlled descent. Perhaps if the day came to use the technique, at a lower altitude things might improve, but the margin for error was tight.

There were a number of features that endeared this aeroplane to pilots, it was as strong as an ox, well balanced, faster than the previous aeroplanes I had flown and for the crews very comfortable and spacious especially for the navigator and the wireless operator. The cockpit area was upholstered with insulating material therefore inside, things were much warmer, instruments better placed for ease of viewing, the controls for auxiliary functions, readily to hand and grouped in a sensible fashion as if they were an integral part of the pilot's office. The tricycle undercarriage was also a new feature, which I took a liking to at once, it made life easier when taxi-ing on the way to the runway, or to the parking area. Of course the level altitude gave better visibility on take off and a quicker acceleration to lift off speed.

The brakes were hydraulically powered and operated by foot pedals, integral with the rudder pedals, many of these features described, would in future years become standard practice in aircraft design. The power was handled by two huge four-bladed propellers of twelve feet or so diameter, and thereby hangs another tale. These propellers were electrically controlled, much as the Wellington's, Dowty Rotol props were, but the Marauder's propellers had a tendency to revert to fine pitch at critical engine speeds, most commonly during the take-off run.

Although the requirement for take off is fine pitch, these guys seemed to have an extra condition of their own, we pilots called it a 'runaway prop,' since the engine revolutions, which are normally held to a constant speed by the propellers mechanism, would rise dramatically, perhaps to four thousand revs per minute, far away in excess of the take off revolutions with the consequent loss of power in that particular engine. Sitting in the Sgt's. Mess we often heard the unmistakable scream of a 'run-away prop' down on the airfield and silently prayed for the safety of the crew. The remedy was to make a quick grab for the pitch control switch, and lower the revs, and put to 'Lock.' This was drastic, but not accomplished without some problems.

The need for an assistant in the right hand seat was never more apparent than in this circumstance, it was virtually impossible to take the action required on one's own, the demands on the pilot, at take off were high enough anyway. The O/C Flying solved our needs by drafting in a number of flight engineers, some Polish who were on rest between tours of ops. or South African Air Force from the training schools in the Nile delta. It was not until I arrived back at Oujda, that I learned of the reason for my conversion course onto Marauders. We had lost several Marauder pilots in an accident at Castel Benito, and were reduced to two qualified pilots, With the others from the course I had attended we now boasted six, enough, since we did not have too many of these aeroplanes to deliver, however, 'another string to my bow' says I.

September bowed out on my return to base, not much to show for 30 days, one Wimpy to Blida, four days flying on conversion total of seventeen hours, plus Cairo and back - twenty eight hours and a few days off between events.

CHAPTER NINE

The promotion system in the RAF, was to say the least, unusual. In the ground trades it was necessary to have the 'time' in, plus, achieving a higher grade in a trade test, then the wait for a vacancy on a unit wherever it may be located. For air crews it was based on time service only, so, after one year as Sergeant, one was promoted to Flight Sergeant, automatically, one year later to Warrant Officer. At any time during one's career, it was possible to apply to be considered for a Commission. Some of our companions did so with varying results, but generally the Nco's stuck together with a blind camaraderie, of better a W/o in the Sergeants Mess than a Pilot Officer in the Officer's Mess. In our Mess things were very unlike an operational unit, the changes of personnel, due to fatalities, was minimal, therefore we began to get top heavy with F/sgts and W/os.

The promotion had a great side effect, that was the increase in pay which went with it, as a Sgt. I was receiving twelve shillings and six pence per day plus two shillings and six pence flying pay. Five pounds five shillings per week, out of which I sent home two pounds ten shillings to which the Air Force added to make up to four pounds something per week. My promotion to F/Sgt. did not come through until August, five months late. As was custom, we had to have a party where the drinks were on me out of the back pay I received. The Sgt's. Mess was run by a small committee of Nco's with a W/o as president of the Mess, ours was a tubby Single's pilot whose main claim to fame was the occasion when he talked whoever was in charge, in the flight office, into allowing him to have a local conversion on to Mosquitoes.

He always took the opportunity to boast of his piloting skills especially when flying a Spitfire, how he would whip the wheels up almost immediately after take off. He had a couple of dual flights and went solo alright, but on his first delivery, with great bravado, he goes into his usual routine and before climbing away, pulled up the wheels too early, the Mossie didn't like it, sank back toward the runway before lifting away. Not before the propellers had struck the ground and about a foot or more of the wooden blades had sheered off, the engines screamed as the revs. went up and he slewed along the ground in a very undignified fashion. How he succeeded in his defence in his Court Martial, I have no recollection, but one very foolish fellow left, never to return to our unit.

You would expect, that having spent the resources on sending me down to Egypt for the Con. course, the O.C. ops. would have work on Marauders lined up for me, not so, it was almost a month until I had the pleasure of taking Mac and Frankie on their first trip in the Marauder. Meanwhile it was a case of business as usual, Wellingtons, Warwicks, etc. with our first introduction to Malta.

Malta a pretty sight from the air on a fine sunny afternoon, the setting sun making the stony island appear as a golden jewel in the blueness of the surrounding sea. The aeroplane safely in the hands of the Air/sea Rescue Squadron at Halfar, we went over to Luqa to seek a ride back to the mainland. What a sight of wreckage and bomb damage, the runway was OK even though it still showed its repair marks, but the buildings -- almost total destruction -- patched up for the umpteenth time, makeshift every thing. The truck which took us into Valetta, made a tortuous route through the rocks and craters, which had caused detours to the roads, passed houses, churches, and other badly damaged buildings where people were staying with their few belongings that had survived the onslaught three years earlier. In the city the damage was even worse, parts had been bombed time after time until there was just ground up rock no bigger than hardcore. Where the buildings were repairable things were brighter, patched shop windows showed off the few things they had to sell, the churches were under repair with masons attempting the impossible, to restore to their glory the treasures of the city.

After the guided tour so to speak, the target of our trip into town was to see the street called 'the Gut' by the Royal Navy, but in fact named 'Strait street.' Here were all the bars and clip joints, where it was custom to start at the top calling at several bars as you made your way down until you reached the waterfront where the Navy liberty boats collected their 'waifs and strays,' in various stages of intoxication, to return them to their ships, for ourselves it was the climb back up the steps to the top to Floriana to ride back to Luqa in the jolting truck on the benches which afforded no comfort.

Also during October there were a few 'Milk Runs,' to do, one minor to Oran from Oujda, ferrying the 'doc' with a patient who needed an operation, and a trip to Casablanca with ten passengers, all Singles pilots, who I was taking there to collect Fighter aeroplanes to deliver. There was an MU. based at Casablance whose job it was to assemble fighters sent out in crates, the same as they did at Takoradi in earlier days. As we approached the airfield, it was so routine that one would not believe what was about to happen, all landing checks completed and satisfactory, the down wind procedure carried out, the passengers warned that we were about to land. Fuel gauges, temperatures every mortal thing checked, no hitches no problems. I turned on to the Finals, informed the tower as normal, and settled the aeroplane down on the runway, after a good approach and landing.

Mac was in the second pilot's seat, and assisting as usual, when I tried to slow down using the brakes in the usual fashion, no response! I called out 'Check air gauges,' 'OK,' from Mac. I had a swift glance at the dials they showed full pressure but no joy from the brakes. 'No brakes,' I yelled not knowing the intercom was on and the VHF on 'transmit,' there wasn't much time or room to waste, the aeroplane was slowing down but would reach the end of the runway before stopping, there was sand at the end of the runway and if I had to, I would raise the wheels when on the sand if the aeroplane did not stop.

Things are never what they seem, all good plans fail sometimes, around the perimeter at about a hundred feet intervals stood empty fifty gallon oil drums painted with black and white hoops acting as markers, I was aiming to avoid these by rudder control or a blip of engine power. Mac had his feet on the instrument panel, his arms across his face, after releasing the escape hatch over the cockpit, and they told me one of the passengers who had plugged into the intercom, overhearing our cries up front, had warned the others at the back, so they took up 'crash stations.' I got the line right we rolled through the gap at about fifty five knots on to the sand. Great, I thought we are in the clear, then it happened! The right wheel dropped into a concrete culvert running diagonally from our right, the right under-carriage leg tore off complete with wheel, the right hand wing tip dropped to the sand and the aeroplane spun to the right.

Unknown to us the American base Fire truck was charging along the runway after us, with the 'Blood Wagon' in attendance, they had heard all the cockpit chat over the intercom. We stopped in a cloud of flying sand, with Mac, big fella he was, forcing his bulk through the hatch, the passengers one after another pouring out through the open Astrodome hatch, whilst I am turning off the fuel pumps, fuel cocks, ignition switches and trying to free Frankie whose door into the cockpit was jammed, a big boot shifted that. We were all out in a couple of minutes, all thirteen of us, unlucky or LUCKY! thirteen, not a scratch, no fire all safe, the Yanks stood goggle eyed at the stream of people getting out of that aeroplane. It was deemed to be 'Pilot error,' at the subsequent enquiry. But with help from the Technical Officer at Casablanca's MU. we established the cause of the brake failure as a faulty valve on the control column. There after an apology appeared in the next Monthly accident report clearing the stigma of 'pilot error' from my records.

CHAPTER TEN

The month ran out with a trip to Castel Benito on a routine ferry flight, by 'Wimpy,' with another crew to fly a Marauder to the Maintenance Unit at Blida, where it was to undergo a major overhaul. It was an aircraft that was on the return to the MU. from a front line Squadron, when it broke down, on the way to Egypt. Having been repaired at Castel Benito by the Duty crew on the staging post, we had the job to fly it up to Blida. It was a crippled old lady without the 'necessary' to get us over the mountains by the direct route. We took a route via El Aouina, at Bizerte, in north east Tunisia. I flew virtually due north up the coast which in those days was almost deserted, just tiny fishing villages clinging to the coast line strip, where today the holiday resorts flourish at Hammamet, Sousse and Gabes. The November weather was deteriorating and conditions forced us to night stop at Bizerte, in fact two nights, guests of the American Air Force, who were always generous with their hospitality. But let me include here a tale of one guy's experience at this airfield.

The incident at El Aouina when Ray Godfrey went in with a Marauder was not so typical of the USAF people. Ray arrived over the airfield at about fifteen hundred feet and looking down at the signals square saw the arrow for a westerly landing direction he radioed to the tower but the controller did not acknowledge Ray's call, however he started his approach and was surprised to have a red Very flare shot up to warn him off landing, so good boy that he was he went round again. Twice more this happened without verbal comment from the ground and no reason as far as he could see, then on the fourth attempt a voice from the control tower asked in a strong Yankee accent 'Whose is that goddamn B26 coming in.' Ray in his best imitation of a Yank replied, 'This is Godfrey's ship and Godfrey bringing her in,' the tower taken aback by the response said, 'Oh, OK bud clear to land.' No reason given but later Ray learned that the direction sign in the signal square was never used at this airfield and Ray was trying to land down wind. So much for the courtesies of the controllers.

So, the following morning well stocked out with Hershey bars and cigarettes, Luckies and Philip Morris in carton loads from the P.X. we set off for Blida, in very poor visibility through driving rain and a hefty head wind. There was no choice of the route, it had to be below cloud at about five hundred feet, following the coast line or at least paralleling it often at the limit of our visibility. I had a F/Sgt Harris flying co-pilot with me and we shared the piloting as we needed a sharp lookout up ahead, for oncoming traffic. I must say that Frankie was in his element with the new set up, the Yankee radios were the same as was used in the Hudson, so he was familiar with these Bendix sets. Mac had little or no navigating to do at this altitude. We did manage a few bearings from Sardinia, at Elmas or the radio station on the extreme southerly point, but they were not too accurate because of the low height at which we were flying, they did at least indicate our progress along the westerly line we were taking. At two hours into the flight the cloud was down so low I called the tower at Bone who offered a guided approach and recommended that we divert to them, since the weather ahead was getting much worse, remember 'do not hazard' the aeroplane on ferry flights. Bone, it was then, landing on the planked runway close to the shore line was an interesting one to be repeated later, on flights into Italy.

The month ended at base, after dropping the tired old Marauder off at the MU. with news that I and my crew were to be posted forthwith to Blida, from whence we had just arrived. At Blida we joined No. 3 Ferry Unit Detachment, which being based at the same airfield as the Maintenance Unit, cut out some of the to-ing and fro-ing in Dakotas. Plus some chances to do air testing after repairs had been carried out. Also Blida was a much larger city than Oujda and of course we were now in Algeria, the truck ride into Algiers the capital was about an hour, and there were Service Clubs where they had films, dances, and ENSA shows, again if one could get in the good books of some Yankee unit, good rations! We had our own Mess entirely air crew, we lived in the former married quarters of the French Air force, two to a room, six to each bungalow with our own kitchen area and wash room, unfortunately cold water only, who needs hot in Africa?

Before reaching yet another Christmas in foreign parts, November and December were varied in the demands made on myself and crew, Cairo was now nine hours away but still about twelve coming back, and also we were now delivering to Sicily, landing at Catania. Here No. 4 Ferry Unit had a detachment to continue the flight to the units in Italy. The wintry weather in the northern Mediterranean contrasted with relatively fine and clear conditions on the desert run, over the sea it often was necessary to fly low perhaps down at one hundred feet or so, to avoid the need to let down through cloud near the Sicilian coast line, and the knowledge that Mount Etna rose to at least ten thousand feet above sea level. The monthly summaries in my log book began to list several types of aircraft flown, Wellington, Hudson, Marauder, Warwick, Ventura, an up grade on the Hudson, Anson and the inevitable passenger rides in the Dakota. Incidentally I learned to play Bridge on the long flights back from Cairo, or Catania. Our Mess sported two or three bridge schools as well as the usual poker school. Pay was lost or prizes gained at these events; not being a gambling man, I managed to keep out of the heavy stakes and stayed solvent.

Christmas seemed suddenly upon us and our puny Mess funds did not run to a special dinner and goodies, the Mess committee did however strike up a deal with the MU. Sgt's. that we should joint them for Christmas dinner and enjoy the hospitality of their Mess on payment of ten shillings per head, money well spent! The meal although tinned turkey was a credit to the cooks, the Italian POW's waited at table, and every one toasted the King. The Mess President read out the Commanding Officer's greetings, the mail had reached us from home all great stuff. Later in the bar I was with my friend from Coventry my home town, Ray Godfrey who I had met by coincidence at Oujda. I had come across his name and service number on the duty board in the ops. room, his number was almost the same as mine, just fifty different in the last three digits. I reasoned that he must have enrolled on the same day as myself at Birmingham, when we went before the selection board, and maybe he was from Coventry too. Sure enough, he had lived close to Coventry Cathedral in the city centre, we became bosom pals, bridge partners, drinking buddies, we even flew down the route in formation on occasions. When he converted to Marauders we had some of our best escapades, together with his wireless Operator, Sgt. Wilkinson who was 'as mad as a hatter' we could paint the town red any time you cared to choose. This Christmas afternoon we settled in easy chairs near the fire of blazing logs and bent the elbows at regular intervals. A very good time was enjoyed by all that day.

The night was rounded off by pooling all our francs and buying bottles of champagne at the equivalent of eight shillings per bottle, with our W/ops we cleared four bottles between us and still were steady enough to walk through the camp back to our quarters. What a different outcome to the Christmas party at Nutts Corner a year earlier. I see that on December 28th we took to the air possibly for the last flight of the year to deliver a Warwick, but after just a few minutes in the air there were problems causing me to return to base and put the aeroplane 'unserviceable' thus ended 1944.

To start a new year it would be nice to relate that we were detailed to make some memorable flight, to an exotic location, the interesting point about the delivery of Warwick BV. 521 to Catania, was we were asked to go via Malta to drop off a passenger, then continue to Sicily. The weather had been pretty appalling for days, and still on the landing fields we were to use, there was not as yet any form of radar assistance for landing. A few beam systems were set up by the Yanks, but only at those sites used by the American Air Transport Command. It was necessary to have good conditions if we were to meet the criteria laid down for the safety of the aircraft, but the passenger on this occasion was a Naval Commander Eckersley-Maslin, who was needed in Malta urgently. It is interesting the records show only, that Blida to Luqa took three hours forty minutes, no comments added, but the   majority of the time in the air was spent flying at low level under the weather, with the Comdr. insisting on sitting in the right hand seat, all fine along the Algerian coast and through Tunisia's northern strip, but come the run over the Med. at about one hundred feet in rain, at too low a level to receive radio signals. It was decidedly unpleasant, we missed pranging on Pantelleria and Lampedusa tiny islands between Tunisia and Sicily on the route to Malta. I finally climbed into the base of the cloud where we started to ice up, unbelievable! but radio signals between ourselves and Luqa were now possible. From them I was able to get a course to steer for the aerodrome, the weather prevailing there, and a talk-in by radio for the approach to the runway. Safely on the ground to the delight of the Naval Commander, who had not enjoyed the flight at all, we drove to the tower to report in, where a jeep was awaiting the Officer, he however dived into his valise and produced like an old fashioned magician, two bottles, one of gin and another of whisky for the crew. Since only Frankie and I were on this flight we took a bottle each, good for a barter with some one one day or lubricate the throat more likely.

Because of the poor weather we were stuck in Malta for two nights before continuing to Catania The return to Algiers by USAAF, C.47 via Palermo took six hours and fifty five minutes, this obsession with lost time, was with me all through the time I spent out there. One could control to some extent the time spent taking an aeroplane out, but the return journey was out of our hands. This return with the Yanks, landing at Palermo was an experience, the runway at the airfield was at right angles to the coast and the inland end faced a mountain, quite close in, sufficiently so that the landing run was made from the sea end and the take off toward the sea. Not only that worry, but the land between the sea and the runway had a distinct slope down toward the airfield, which gave the impression that the aeroplane was kind of 'surfing' along the fields with their dry stone walls around them. Great in summer maybe but in thick 'clagg' no joy at all. That day we got down, without scaring the pants off us, but the next leg was a weirdo, low level across the Med. at about fifty to one hundred feet in a Dakota bobbing and weaving through the muck and rain. As a passenger you have no chance to do anything on your own behalf, when one is a Pilot to boot, it's worse.

CHAPTER ELEVEN

In mid January, we got our own personal Flight Engineer, he was from South Africa, Port Elizabeth, and called Ken Nolte, he was a Sergeant. He came with high references from the training school in Palestine, but he had qualified on Liberators, and we had a spell of training for him to do on the Marauder, Mac and Frankie would put him right with much of the aircraft systems.

Ken joined the crew when we were beginning to make deliveries direct to squadrons in Italy, or forward maintenance units, so now we were faced with weather conditions much different to the desert conditions that we were used to, Northern Italy in winter is much like in Britain, very cold both day and night. Low pressure systems prevailed in the north stretching to southern Sicily, hence some of the diabolic rain and low cloud we had suffered throughout December and January. Minus 10 F. was not uncommon, and low level fog could cause trouble when attempting to reach Foggia in central Italy. The mountains forming the backbone of Italy called the Apennines, run for 800 miles from the north to the tip in the south, are up to nine thousand feet in height and made for us another hurdle to overcome in bad weather. On days with heavy cloud down to low levels it might not be possible to go over the top, when our favoured route would be direct from Algiers to the Naples area, then over to the Adriatic. When fine no problem, just climb to ten thousand feet plus, and let down through the cloud breaks, but in dirtier stuff provided the eastern side was relatively clear it was possible to reach a point, by dead reckoning, over the airfields around Foggia, and request homings at intervals until they were westerly headings to steer for the field, then continuing to the east, one could let down through the overcast in the knowledge that one was over the coastal plain and clear of the mountains. In the winter of 1944/5 this was our only way over, to get the aeroplanes through being more important than ever, because of 'the round the clock' attacks on Rumania and southern Germany.

If we needed a flight home from Foggia it was necessary to cadge a lift to Naples, Capodichino, from where the American Air Transport Command ran regular flights to Algiers and beyond. There was also a Transit hotel in Naples used by all the British Forces in transit, it was often the case that a flight was booked up, and our passes did not give the same rights of precedence with the Americans, as they did with the British, so with a day to spare, into Naples it would be. The poverty was unbelievable, ragged urchins begging on the main streets, the Americans supporting the Black market with their cigarettes, food etc. from the P.X., there were areas of the city in which one did not feel safe at all, on the other hand the sea front parks were resplendent still with the Roman statues untouched.

For entertainment there were a few cinemas showing old Hollywood movies, dubbed with Italian dialogue and occasionally subtitled in Italian or English as appropriate. The Forces Clubs were quite good and were well patronised by all ranks, and of course after hours there seemed to be the inevitable inter Service brawl, which could turn nasty, so it was best not to stay late. The region above the city, was cooler, here the more well-to-do people lived and here also a few reasonable restaurants where with a bit of luck you might get something resembling a decent meal. One evening three of us, managed to get seats in the San Carlo Opera house to see 'Rigoletto'. As my first visit to the opera, I was converted to the fact that opera was for anyone, the settings were marvellous, and although I could not understand the words, I was able to follow the plot, the cast were terrific, I had never heard singing like this.

The opera house was a magnificent building, unspoiled by war and apparently getting back to normal business, just like the theatres did in London after the Blitz. The interior was breathtakingly beautiful, mainly red drapes, the ceilings painted and gilded. The cast made a splendid evening of it, I would like to think that it made such an impression on me that I was to become a devotee of opera, but not so, although I do enjoy occasionally a visit to see a touring opera.

Always present in the background to Naples is Vesuvius, the volcano near the remains of Pompeii, the Roman town swamped by a deluge of larva when Vesuvius erupted in AD 79, and by coincidence it had done so again in 1944, the red cloud of smoke rose several thousand feet into the air. It was RAF instructions to forbid any aircraft from entering the cloud since it was heavily polluted with volcanic ash which was harmful to the internals of the engines. It was quite an awesome sight even when seen from a fair distance, it seemed to be active for months on end. Well into the next year.

The winter was still on when I had to take a Marauder to a squadron based in the north of Italy, on an airfield at Iesi, near Falconara. Again the cloud base was very low, so a coastal run took us as far as Bone, where after a consultation with the Met. man it was suggested that to go via Sardinia might prove better. It would be a low level run again, relying on Radio homings from Elmas, the airfield built by, the Italians for the city of Cagiliari. The time taken was just one hour but the strain of low flying made it seem longer, the route could not be made direct since the outcrop of hills to the south west of the island caused us to fly easterly until the headings given by Elmas radio were 20 degrees off to the west of north. A night stop, there, then to Pomigliano close to the slopes of Vesuvius, for another weather check, then over the mountains to Biferno. The night stop here was to allow an early start on the next day, avoiding night flying since the days were now so short, and because we would need a truck ride to Falconara to get transport back to Naples, and home to Algiers.

The following day was bright but very cold, the short flight to Iesi lasted one hour, on the approach I was warned of ice on the runway, such as it was, and to take care, as if I needed reminding. Our unit took in five new Marauders that morning, the squadron were gathering around almost as soon as we landed, they were to change to the Marauder from their present aircraft, and wanted to know as much as we could tell them about the aeroplane. Ridiculous Ferry Pilots teaching Bomber crews, what did we know about action, however we could at least generalise, and allay some fears of the aeroplanes former reputation. We spent a while in the Sgt's Mess chatting to the crews and having some food. Glib words to describe a new experience, off the airfield the ground was now a sea of mud as the overnight frost thawed, the jeep taking the crews to the Mess slithered and slid all over the place. The 'Mess' was a bombed out building, furnished with whatever the guys could find or appropriate, it did not have any heating, all the men were wearing as much of their clothing that they could get into, but they treated us right royally with food and drink, and since the weather further north was not fit for ops. they decided to 'raise the roof' on behalf of their visitors. The truck ride to Falconara was 'interesting,' if you were bothered to raise a bleary eye to look out.

Even at the end of January we were terminating flights and turning back because of the weather, but my crew and I managed to take out six aeroplanes despite the conditions. To people of today, the latter part of the century, the facilities we had fifty years ago for blind flying were primitive to say the least. Hence the continual harping on about the weather, we could not get down, even if we got up on the top. That trip to Iesi took a total time of six and a half hours over a three day period, the return to Maison Blanche at Algiers, two separate trips by Dakota, Falconara to Naples, then on to Algiers the next day, six and a quarter hours. One aeroplane delivered over five days, and thirteen hours in the air doesn't seem very efficient looking back, but then the aids were limited and the aircraft were slow.

January saw the promotion of Ted McKenzie to Pilot Officer, he had done his time admirably and deserved the rise in status, Frank Allaire was already a Warrant Officer, having completed the two years required, and was now waiting for the commissioning board to review his application. Mac's departure to the Officer's Mess was a great loss to the Sgt's, he had been the life and soul of the Mess on social evenings and a great supporter of the bridge school, we missed his company on the ground. In the air there was no difference in our relationships he was still the navigator, I was still the skipper, and so was Frank, still the wireless operator, we respected each other's skill and acknowledged it, and the frivolous attitude to all things official, often spilled over into pranks not always accepted when in the air. From the early days flying down the route, Mac had made notes of many features on the ground, that struck him as useful to the future journeys over the same terrain. To the untrained eye there was nothing of special interest to be made note of, however two white houses in the midst of the desert scrub, making an unusual pattern were enough for this wizard of the nav. charts to highlight for future use, he would get Frank to obtain two or, possibly three bearings, so that he could fix the exact location, and plot it.

At one stage the orders came down from Group that they wanted to see the Navigators producing a completed log for every flight, no more of your 'back of fag packet' navigation, each flight log would need to have a minimum number of fixes, wind speed and drift calculations per hour, some kind of assessment of their work load and industriousness, it was supposed, by the cynical amongst us. The same edict applied to the W/ops, a minimum number of requests for bearings to be made per hour, to assist the navigators, so many D.F. readings per hour, weather report requests etc. there was near revolution for a couple of months or so, until it died a natural death.

There was of course a lighter side to flying as well as the serious, such as visiting the 'loo,' a chemical toilet bolted to the floor three quarters of the way back toward the rear turret. With a bit of twisting, and leaning to the right it was possible to see from the pilot's seat through the length of the fuselage to the back end. I had devised a welcoming procedure for any likely users of the Elsan, as they prepared to squat down I would either kick on full rudder or push the control column to cause the loo to effectively lurch away, or rise up swiftly catching the unfortunate guy literally 'with his pants down,' you don't pull that stunt very often without some retaliation.

Mac's method was to return to the cockpit and peer out to the front as if searching for a landmark, then when I was off guard he would turn off a petrol cock on the central pedestal, make some remark about the progress we were making or a small change to our course to steer, enough to put me at ease with the world, until the engine on the fuel starved side would cut out, I should say he only pulled this stunt at a safe height. There would be a few minutes panic as I tried to decide the reason for the failure, quickly switching on the booster pumps, selecting cross-feed, straightening the aeroplane, applying trim etc. then in a quieter vein, try to assess what had happened. I'll admit the first time he did this I nearly died on the spot, expecting to have to put down on the desert quite a distance south of Tobruk. An alternative but with a much more immediate effect, was to switch off the magnetos on one side or just pull back a throttle, neither of which were as dramatic as turning off the fuel.

On the ground there were other pranks taking place, the drivers of the jeeps with the FOLLOW ME signs on the back were fair game for a joke or two. They would come out to the end of the runway where the aircraft turned off ready to taxi, the signs could be illuminated and below the Follow Me was another saying Stop. The trick was to slowly increase speed as you followed, and the poor driver found himself racing away to avoid the pilot who seemed hell bent on chopping up the jeep with the propellers. In a tricycle undercarriage aircraft with good visibility, we often got up to nearly forty mph around the perimeter track with the driver flashing the stop sign on and off. I guess our normal speed was perhaps ten or twelve mph. The faces of the drivers was distinctly ashen when we reached the apron. There was always the chance that the controller would witness the incident but rarely was there any reaction, as I said a bit of a joke.

In February 1945 I pulled another stunt on a fellow pilot, I was detailed to accompany F/o Mayo in an Anson taking five pilots from Blida to Setif, an MU. up in the mountains south of Bone, they were to collect six Bostons and return them to Blida. I was given the job of flying the Anson back home. I was not conversant with the Anson other than in a passenger role on nav. flights. Neither was I cleared to fly the Boston but that was not to be a hurdle. I had long had a desire to fly this machine and was well clued up as to the various safety speeds, flap settings etc. On landing at Setif I climbed into the jeep and we sped off to the dispatch tent, I signed the '700' and drove out to the flight line to climb into the aeroplane, the mechanic lay on the wing beside the cockpit to help with starting. I felt around at the various levers memorising which was which and having got clearance to taxi, proceeded to the end of the runway. At Setif the runway had two massive steps in the first and second third of its length, going east were drops of about ten feet over a relatively short distance. You could be fooled into believing that you were properly airborne, when suddenly you struck the ground again. A story goes that a newcomer to Setif was taking off and after rising off the second drop, he raised the wheels assuming he was now airborne only for the aeroplane to drop back down, the propellers struck the runway breaking up as did that 'Mossie' at Blida, but sadly as the propellers on a Wimpy were in direct line with the cockpit, a large chunk of debris shot inside through the side of the cockpit and killed the pilot, the aeroplane crashed, the others escaped.

I contemplated the Setif runway as I waited for clearance to take off, reaching for full throttle when lined up, the acceleration of the Boston was something different to any other aeroplane I had flown, I was solo on this flight so was able to enjoy the experience just like those earlier days during training, in Canada when you go solo for the first time. The take off proved no problem, it was a trifle confusing since it wasn't possible to see all of the controls, as a number were positioned on the bulkhead behind the pilot, who was able to reach them on either side of the seat. This was the reason for the varied shapes of the knobs on the control levers, they all meant something to me in those days, undercarriage, cowl gills, flaps etc. Ernie Robinson a colleague, had suggested some throttle and pitch settings, not those in the Pilot's Notes, he had given his opinion as to the approach speed to adopt with and before extending flaps. We used to have a saying 'approach speed from the book plus 5 mph for the wife, 5 mph for mother and another 5 mph for luck,' this could put the speed up by 20% too much really. On the circuit at Blida I was given clearance to land, made all the right moves did the landing drills on the down wind leg, turned on to finals with a little flap and at 130 mph as discussed with Ernie Robinson earlier, the runway was coming up at a hell of a rate. At about 150 feet I selected full flaps, began the flare out, and touched down neatly, but the aeroplane was using up runway at a great rate, with only yards to spare, I managed to turn at the end onto the perimeter track and stop. So much for the extra insurance, stick to the book in future. Of course I was in the proverbial again, but since we now had a new C.O. I got the Boston added to my log book along with the others.

CHAPTER TWELVE

After two Boston deliveries, and a row with F/O Mayo over the Setif incident, I received orders to go to 1330 Conversion Unit forthwith to convert to Liberators, the American B24, four engined bomber, this aircraft was coming through in numbers and the squadrons in Italy were re-equipping with them. I was one of a team of eight pilots who went to Bilbeis to train on them for ferrying. The system of instruction had not changed, class work first, to learn the systems on board, the emergency procedures, hydraulics, electrics, auto-pilot, etc. etc. took about seven days with visits to the hangars to view the aeroplane at first hand. On arrival at the flight office I was met by Chris Bland who now held the post as Chief Flying Instructor, and also in my case the instructor with whom I would learn to fly the Liberator. It would be fun to say that we had some excitement but it was now routine to change from one aircraft to another, we would fly in two or three hour stints sharing the time between two training pilots who alternated as first or second pilot, learning the procedures for each seat. Peter Powell from Blida flew several times with myself, under the guidance of Chris Bland. Peter was one of the longest serving pilots on 3 Ferry unit, taking residence in Oujda in 1943. After four hours 'flying on circuits and bumps' plus simulated engine failure, and then flying on three or even two engines, we were allowed to fly the left hand seat, without the instructor on board. We built up our experience by flying twice each day. The handling of this big bird was incredible and the performance on two engines, both 'dead' ones out on the same side had to be experienced to be believed, the manoeuvrability had us amazed.

One particular day I was in the left seat and initiating the take off run, I had done all the drill for take off and commenced the run down the runway, the aeroplane reached take off speed but wasn't responding. It showed no sign of lifting off, the end of the runway was getting near and there was every indication that we were due for a bad situation on the rapidly approaching sand when she gently rose into the air. Sighing with relief I climbed away calling for 'wheels up' reset the throttles and pitch for climb, trimmed out the aeroplane then, at a safe 500 ft. called 'Flaps up.' The second pilot replied 'Flaps already up.' It was now obvious why the aeroplane was so reluctant to take off, we had missed the flaps in the pre-flight check at the end of the runway. I turned to Ray Godfrey, who had come along for the ride, 'had he noticed our mistake?' Of course he had but did not want to upset anyone, he would like to see what was going to happen. Stupid clot! we could have had a nasty time, it was bad enough as it was, we were fortunate that the aeroplane was lightly loaded with less than half its normal fuel load, it was essential to use 15 degrees of flap for any take off. One other highlight was the opportunity to make a three engined landing, admittedly with the instructor on board, but you did the flying yourself, the air-space at Bilbeis was too crowded with smaller aeroplanes, so we were directed to Cairo West out on the fringe of the desert with its long runways, and long spells during the day without a great deal of traffic. This seemed heaviest late at night for outgoing and early evening for incoming, therefore we had the airfield almost to ourselves.

In the evenings it was a case of study or entertain oneself in the mess, which was quite a small place dolled up a shade Hawaiian style, at least if the cinema is to be believed. Shooting Poker dice was a popular way of losing your money, and the Station Warrant Officer, an older man of long service in the RAF, reckoned he was 'hot stuff' with the dice. Every night he was propping up the bar, with a drink near at hand which didn't seem to diminish. He tried riling newcomers, but failed with Ray Godfrey who seemed unafraid of anyone. The gauntlet was thrown down and the fight was on, neither liked each other, even though they had only met two weeks before, they played into the small hours for three nights running. Ray took him for about fifty pounds Egyptian, just what Ray needed. I'm afraid W.O. Porter had met his match that time.

The course over, it was favourite to have a couple of nights in Cairo, I usually stayed at Rhodesia House, a club set up for Rhodesian forces, which welcomed us 'Limey's' unlike the Anzac or Kiwi Clubs who only wanted their own. There was nothing for the British. Around the corner was a Club called the Washington, a clean and pleasant place, with a cabaret spot complete with belly dancer, it was a good show they put on. The drinks were reasonably priced and genuine, not watered down rubbish found in some places. Malta being a very bad example of bar keepers swindling the Tommies or Jack ashore off his ship.

The Air Booking Centre was the first port of call, the next morning, with the request, that they do not put themselves out, to fit us into their overloaded schedule we can wait another night. Damned generous of us. We were after all just a bunch of 'skivers' looking for the chance to make the best of the war, chances abounded in Cairo, to get your haircut, have some alterations made to your 'issue' shirts or especially, the issue shorts. These revolting objects came down to your knees almost, had three short belts at the wait to buckle across, we favoured the Australian style, half thigh length and sports style waist. The most popular shirt was the 'Bush jacket' or Safari style, we would go to any lengths to get a couple of these, in Cairo it was possible to have any sort of clothing tailor made within twenty four hours, for a few shillings a time. The people in Rhodesia House brought in the tailor who took the measurements, then haggled over the price and finally dashed away with the promise, to be back before one left to fly back. The most important piece of kit was the boots, they had to be pukka desert boots made of camel hide, suede side out and with the genuine 'brothel creeper' soles, soft sponge rubber on a leather base. The official RAF mosquito boots were not bad either, but since they were for evening use in the mess, their prime task was to keep the mosquitoes at bay from the ankles, they were not very durable, also not à la mode, don't you know. Maybe the desert fever was taking us over a shade, we used to reckon that the heat did get to you in the end. As the Brummies say 'Any road up' it was back to Blida, after a month away again, what changes this time, perhaps the best was yet to come.

March in Algeria, is a new season, starting to improve as far as the weather is concerned, gone are the heavy thick clouds and the sun begins to predominate, the war was reaching a peak, and the aircraft were in great demand. We started with a Liberator Mark VI destined for Foggia, a straightforward flight of four hours thirty minutes, clear air, direct from Maison Blanche, then over the top, near Naples and Benevento. The new VHF sets gave a greater range than the older models, so I was able to receive airfield information earlier than previously and plan the approach in a better manner. This time, as we began to near the aerodrome, the tower asked if we would stand-off at ten thousand feet to allow a large formation of American Fortresses and Liberators to land on the cluster of airfields, surrounding Foggia.

We peered out to the east and saw this huge mass of aircraft making their way back into their nesting places, there were ragged holes in what had been a tight formation, I supposed, on their way out earlier that day. Some were flying on less than the full four engines, a few trailing smoke or oil vapour behind them, as we circled out over the Adriatic, we watched as the stragglers came home at low level, nursing the cripples back, a truly moving sight. The delay was no hassle after seeing this armada of aircraft arriving at their home bases, they had taken a beating.

Our return flight was to take back from the squadron, No. 104 I believe, who had received the Liberator, a well worn 'Wimpy' which had seen much use, it was completely out of trim, and sported a varied array of patches over the wings and fuselage. The poor old thing staggered up to a safe height to cross the mountains, on the way to Pomigiliano, where we ended our day's flying with a night stop. All through the next day's flying, I had the left rudder trim fully over and my left leg stuck out in front as if I was unable to bend it and the control column over the left also to keep up the right wing. That trip lasted four hours back to Blida. I was shattered, although the aeroplane responded magnificently on the landing approach and during the landing itself. Maybe it was pleased to be down also, and recognised it was due to have the best overhaul of its life.

The ground crews groaned when they saw her, 'Why bring that thing back here?' 'Where did you pick up that heap?' was their comment, doubtless they had never had to have the faith in an aircraft, such as the air crews did and praised it through the roof, when returning to base after a particularly bad operational sortie.

There was a distinct lack of Liberators in March, unless someone was keeping their whereabouts secret, we made do with Warwick, Boston, Wellington and Marauder trips to Italy or Cairo. It must have been a busy month I did seventy hours in the air.

Oh yes, I received my promotion to Warrant Officer too, but lost Frankie from the crew after all this time. He was commissioned as a Pilot Officer and went home to Canada. Dennis our navigator who we started out with in Canada, had gone to Malaya, with the former C.O. of our unit, S/Ldr. Hilary, to fly Dakota's on supply dropping missions to the troops with General Slim's forces.

My crew was now a complete mix of people who either wanted to fly with me or suffered in silence, the former I hope. The new recruit to our vacant seat at the radios, was F/Sgt. Cyril Stafford from Essex, married like myself and, with one son, methodical and a trifle serious. He could not be faulted in his work and assistance to the crew.

April signed in, with some of the best weather, and flying we could expect out there, several deliveries to Capodichino near Naples where an advance MU had been established, many types of aircraft were lined up on the airfield, waiting their future destinations. Ken Nolte my flight engineer was keeping his hand in doing landings from the right hand seat, he was very good. It would be up to him to bring in the aeroplane in an emergency. It was all Liberators during April, for all eight captains and their crews even one to Luqa, but, for one exception, in our case, a Warwick Mk. 1 Air-Sea rescue aircraft, complete with its airborne lifeboat. Even with this hung under the fuselage, the aeroplane handled quite normally. So having aborted a flight to Italy, with a Liberator whose generators were giving trouble, after half an hour, from take off and returned to Maison Blanche, on the previous day, we set forth from Blida to take this Warwick to Sardinia, the day was fine, the sun blazing down, feet on the pedestal, radio on, piping music through the intercom, when at thirty minutes out over the sea, the starboard oil pressure gauge showed a significant fall, at the same time the temperature of the oil was rising very rapidly. Reducing power on that engine and opening the cooling gills and oil radiator shutters, did nothing to bring the temperature down. Fearing an engine seizure we, Ken and I, shut down the fuel lines, throttled back and feathered the propeller to reduce the drag on that side. We turned back towards the coastline the handling now was quite difficult, the boat was a consideration if it should be necessary to land wheels up or should any other thing go wrong on landing. Staffy's dream came true, he sent out a May Day call to Maison Blanche informing them of our situation, meanwhile Ken and I concentrated on flying the aeroplane back, and deciding when to ditch the life boat if and when it was necessary.

The navigator on this trip was Sgt. Reynolds, and at his suggestion we reckoned it best policy to drop the boat, close inshore, such that it might be recovered by one of the naval launches from the harbour in Algiers. Wasn't that the reason for the boat in the first place? To be dropped to crews in the water? There were six parachutes to let it down smoothly, I'll admit we didn't have a clue as to the procedure to adopt but 'needs must as circumstances allow.' But struggling back at about four thousand feet on one engine wasn't funny either. We told the airfield of our intention and prepared a plan based on the off-shore wind to drop the boat almost at the high water mark, so whilst drifting down on the parachutes, it would also drift out to shallow water to be recovered easily. The navigator was checking the release gear we assumed that it would be associated with the bomb release gear, no joy there, then they discovered a toggle marked 'Release' and decided that a special bit of kit had been fitted and this was it. We flew back the sixty miles or so toward the airfield, came to the shore line and Bud Reynolds pulled the toggle. Staffy was in the rear checking, nothing going down! What is wrong now? several more tugs at the release, no joy. Why were we not aware of what to do? Then brain wave I reached down to the jettison lever, the one used to jettison the bomb load, down went the boat in all its glory, sporting only two parachutes. Staffy's commentary from the back was hilarious I can't repeat the lurid description, 'the f...ing thing's doing down like a bat out of hell' etc. then 'Shit! It's gone into the roof of a house.'

By no means the end of my story, there's more to come. Even with 700 hours flying to my credit, it was not every day that I would have expected to attempt a single engined landing. It was a long time ago that I was in Training Command, what did I learn? Soon I would have the chance to show whether or not I had. The tower gave clearance to make a direct approach on to finals, that is to say, no circuit before the landing, just come right in, I made the landing checks, adjusted the trims, set throttle settings, pitch, booster pump on, but with only a slight amount of flap, and delayed lowering the wheels to keep the drag down, until the last opportunity. Fine, all correct on the approach, reducing height steadily, at 100 knots, down with the undercarriage, call the tower again, speed down to now 80 knots, a smooth approach everything looking fine. Then whoosh a flight of Yankee fighters are crossing in front of me. Where the hell did they come from? No radio message from them or the tower. I pull upwards trying to stop the descent, and attempting to avoid these invaders on my flight line. Putting on power to the live engine, created a swing to the right, which at around 75 knots, was caused by the levelling out and low speed. I had great difficulty in correcting. I opted for an attempt to make another circuit and abort this landing. It meant raising the wheels and putting on full power, now we were half way along the runway, at its right hand edge, with the speed falling slowly and the aeroplane refusing to climb, it is not recorded who saw us crossing the airfield at such a preposterous altitude, but a Warwick WILL fly at about 60 knots, not very well mind you. How we missed the tents of the ground crews to the right at the end of the runway, was not planned, it was more hope than good judgement, the main road alongside the airfield loomed up. I say loomed, since at this point the aeroplane was down at sixty or seventy feet with one of the local vineyards dead ahead. It was now obvious to a blind man, that we had no choice, I had to put it down. NOW! I throttled back the good engine, this resulted in a little more control, and at about 50 knots with the nose of the aeroplane raised we slid to a standstill amid the young vines, in a cloud of dust, no bones broken, propellers bent and the underside roughed up a bit, safely down.

Not the result I had planned for but at least no injuries and the aeroplane could fly again one day. Of course there would have to be an enquiry set up into the cause of my accident. I would be required to make out a report on what had occurred, my actions and reasons for them, then attend the 'Court of enquiry,' at some future date.

CHAPTER THIRTEEN

The following month the war was over I did not fly a Warwick again, there were other jobs to attend to, flying was going to get a bit thin in the future.

Not quite true, about the Warwick I mean, a few days before VE Day, on May 5th, Bud Reynolds, Staffy and I took off in a Warwick from Blida, but in fifteen minutes we were on the ground again the aircraft having gone U/S with a dickie generator.

The morning following the news of victory, the Station Commander called a parade of all ranks, to declare that the war was officially over, and that from his experience of the end of the First World War, he was a South African Major, and the excited behaviour of the soldiers at that time, he was ordering that all firearms were to be handed into the armoury at once, but that to mark this special day an issue of two bottles of beer, would be made to each man on the unit. The C.O. of 3 Ferry Unit had his say, thanking all the air crews for their dedication to duty, he said their efforts had been essential to the outcome of the war. They had been just as important in their role as the other units of the RAF. Now the boredom would perhaps set in.

In the aftermath of the declaration of peace in Europe and the cessation of hostilities between the Allies and Germany, the lives of our fliers were stood upon their heads, they were literally redundant the very day after they had been the front line of the fighting forces, just because the struggle was over. Yet there appeared to be no plan to deal with the enforced hiatus in which they now found themselves the need for new aircraft was no longer the prime need, all patrols and strikes were finished, transport and coastal assistance such as air sea rescue, were the only reasons for taking to the air.

What to do with the exuberance of youth, now denied an outlet to give out their relief and thankfulness for successfully completing their war service, in the manner of which youth is accustomed, was a question that did not seem to have been considered by the leadership. These young men were in need of guidance, or in today's terms counselling, for the future which after today was going to be that long sought after something that they had only dreamed about and for which they had made no provision whatsoever. The immediate need was to stave off the boredom that would inevitably prevail, with too much free time, totally without a planned approach to its utilisation. What was done in the UK for the likes of us we did not know, but out here the daily routine was to first recover from the night before, take what breakfast one could, collect the mail from home and maybe reply, but all the time with a languor and couldn't care less attitude to everything in authority. We celebrated for several days in the bar, in the Mess in general, the usual steeple chasing over the settees. The poker schools were popular. 'Blondie' Scarbrow spent an entire evening in his underpants, having lost all his money, wagered most of his kit, and his clothes, in the biggest game of the month. There were rituals dreamed up to create distractions from the ever present lassitude, like drinking circles in which one paid premiums into the drinks kitty, the value of the fee dependent on which ring of seats you were occupying, the more senior your rank the closer to the centre ring you sat and the lesser the costs. The group I was in, was intent on drinking only Scotch whisky and due to rationing the allocation had to be shared equally between Canadian and the traditional Scotch brands. Whenever the Canadian was on the bar a suitable sum would be taken from the kitty to buy the whole bottle of Canadian which was ceremoniously thrown from the window to break below then back to the Scotch. What madness but such hilarity and comradeship.

A fortnight later the conversion to Liberators came to be a benefit, several were required in Italy and my crew were granted a couple of weeks rest and leave in Sicily, at Taormina where there was a rest set up in the St. George's hotel. We first took a Liberator from Maison Blanche to Brindisi, via Malta where we drew our pay in pounds, so we were then able to change it into Lira, on the black market in Italy at a better rate than the paymaster gave, approximately twice the standard rate. This had been a ploy used by all crews, draw your pay in Egypt since the Egyptian pound was very stable, and the paymaster rate was 200 francs, or 400 Lira to the pound. All through the Med you could get 400 and 1000 respectively from the back street money changers, great for financing further ventures.

The two weeks in Taormina were fun, days spent on the beaches and swimming in the clearest blue sea I ever saw, a jeep to take the swimmers down the steep road to the shore and return us to the hotel, where we had full waiter service, the food was splendid, fresh fruit and fresh fish, even choices on the menu. We paid dues as if we were in the Mess at base but there the resemblance stopped. We could have tea served on the terrace, choose when to eat and for a change go into the town to one of the bars to enjoy a sing song. In any group there would be someone who could play a musical instrument, piano, clarinet or other. One must remember that it was nearer a village than a conventional English town, and a trip from bar to bar could encompass the whole place in a few minutes. One particular bunch of fliers had a bogus 'ritual' ceremony to perform before any meal, they would begin to chant as if in Arabic or Moslem fashion then call for 'a few words from the Koran,' whereupon one guy would pull out his diary, or other small book and pretend to recite verses, they then followed a ritual seeking of the east using a hand held compass, service issue marching compass. Having found the true direction, they then spread their napkins on the floor very ceremoniously and knelt down to bow to the east, 'Sand happy,' you guessed it in one, time to 'catch the boat that takes me home,' as the song goes. Came the day to return to Blida and there were many long faces.

June saw us deliver to Capodichino, two Liberators, which relieved the inactivity, for a while but after the rushing about over the Mediterranean for two years the pain of not flying was intense. Discipline was breaking down, drinking was on the increase, foolish behaviour was rife. These keyed up young men most less than 23 years of age, needed something to occupy their energies. In July my chance finally came to break out of the tedium, we had eight Liberator pilots, and orders came through that we should take seven Liberators to the UK. Oh joy, going home! The C.O. granted seven days leave to all crews on the delivery run. Also we were to select from a list of crews those people who were almost 'time expired,' that is to say three and a half years for a single chap or two and a half for a married man. The full term was 4 yrs. and 3 yrs. respectively. We worked through a list from the longest serving overseas, to the most recent recruit, to our unit and made up the crews to about seven or eight members. I was to fly second pilot to Jack Masterton, the O/c multi's. We would leave by truck for Maison Blanche and fly the following day, to Melton Mowbray.

It was a bright and beautiful Friday morning as we took off from Maison Blanche's runway at about 6 am. The whole crew at their stations, and the extra 'bods' occupying the vacant seats or the bunks, the forecast was good for the whole of the flight, at around seven thousand feet the visibility was unlimited, as an instance it was not too long after take off that we were able to pick out the Balearic's up to the north east of our position, the sea was tranquil like the proverbial mill 'pond,' and as so often seen on our flights an azure blue as you will ever see again, the winds were favourable, our ETA was around one o'clock in Melton, peace reigned once more, we were on our way home, some after three years in the desert. Great ! Without any enemy to be wary of, the best route was nearly due north, to gain the French coast west of Marseilles.

Across France there began a dressing parade as everyone on board the aeroplane took turns to retire to the compartment at the rear, above the bomb bay, where the kit-bags, or travel bags were stowed. Here we changed into our 'best Blues' from the Khaki drill uniforms worn in Africa. Below were the small fields and the red tiled roofs of the French villages. All were eagerly waiting for the English channel to appear it was to be a longer wait, as far as, some of the more impatient ones were concerned, at our airspeed the time from south to north of France was almost three hours. So it was a case of sit back, eat your sandwiches, listen out for air traffic control, keep an eye on the auto pilot and wait. I believe the inevitable card school started up in the rear, near the waist gunner's ports usually the table would comprise, parachute bags surmounted by a flight bag it was common enough in all flying situations. Jack and I shared the flying and took our turn to go back and change.

The 'blues' which were hardly ever worn in North Africa were uncomfortable and itchy, compared with the light weight khaki. Our track lay to the west of Paris and through patchy cloud we were able to see parts of Normandy and the Seine valley the bombed areas around Rouen showed up, we flew over the fields of Normandy, but were not able to see the beach head areas because of the low stratus cloud. Finally, glimpses of the Channel below reassured us that at long last we were truly going home.

We crossed the coast near Bournemouth at about 12.30 pm. and the green fields of England slid slowly, beneath the nose of the Liberator, approximately an hour to go. Our radio calls to Uxbridge brought replies as to the heights to fly and best route, our briefing in Algiers was rather primitive in respect to Air Traffic rules in the UK. but keeping a constant vigil Jack and I brought the big bird to Melton's runway at about 1.30 after a flight of six and a half hours of uncomplicated and smooth flying. There were shouts of joy from the guys at the rear of the aeroplane when Jack rolled the Lib. onto the deck, while I tidied up the aeroplane, raising the flaps, opening the cooling grills, going through the after landing procedure. We chased the Follow Me jeep around the perimeter track to the apron, and shut down the motors, definitely in England now.

The other aeroplanes began to arrive at intervals through the next hour, all safely in, the crews were gathering in the ops. room, for a basic debrief on the flight, smoking, sitting where they could and drinking mugs of tea supplied by two NAAFI girls. The contrast of the tanned skin of our boys and the locals, was most apparent, I wasn't sure if they were faded or we had changed to brown skins, the difference was so noticeable. With around sixty flight crew sitting in this building, tired, dirty, hungry and desperate to get to the nearest railway station, things weren't going smoothly. A conference was afoot between Jack Masterton and the resident O.C. operations who was trying to insist on the next stage of the delivery flight to take place tomorrow, Saturday, by taking the aeroplanes to Renfrew in Scotland. The passengers who had come along for the ride home and leave, did not wish to travel any further than necessary, they booed and shouted down the S/Ldr. at every opportunity. Jack came to a compromise, we would set the non crew guys on their way immediately they had had some food etc. and the station clerks would provide the Rail warrants as quickly as possible.

We finally waved them off, at around 5 o'clock in the afternoon, as the remaining crew members found a billet for the night and prepared to go into Melton Mowbray as quickly as possible to catch the pubs opening at six o'clock. How we had dreamed of a pint of real beer, and what we were to do when the occasion arose to down several pints of the best Midland ale. Ten minutes to six that evening found four or five Warrant Officers sitting on the doorstep of the Bluebell public house in Melton waiting for 'Mine host' to open up the doors of his establishment to satisfy the needs of his visitors from overseas. Promptly on six o'clock the doors opened, we swaggered in happy to be back, for was this not the self same pub we had drunk in during our last stay at RAF Melton Mowbray. The pints were pulled and to the delight of the landlord, speeches made, extolling the virtues of English beers in general and this brew in particular, greetings exchanged with the locals when they arrived, to see these swarthy members of His Majesties Forces celebrating their homecoming. The first pints didn't touch the sides of our throats on the way down, then 'Fill 'em up landlord' was the repeated call for quite a while, into the later part of the evening. One bloke after downing three pints almost without stopping for air, keeled over and fell flat on his back, it took quite a while to get him to his feet again. We staggered up the lane toward the billets in the summery evening light, not caring a jot for the rest of mankind. We were Home. The beer was as good as always. All's well with the world, next stop bed.

Saturday morning after breakfast, in the Ops. room, a heated discussion was going on between our senior officer and the self same S/Ldr. as the previous afternoon. This time the odds were in our favour, the night before while our group enjoyed the hospitality of the pub, half the crews had sloped off to the railway station and gone home. The lure of their loved ones was too much to resist, the war was over the aeroplanes could wait, until more urgent matters were dealt with. I had only been away eighteen months but some mates had endured almost three years, abroad a veritable lifetime to a twenty two year old. After much wrangling it was obvious that we were under staffed to move the aeroplanes, therefore after re-reading our C.O.'s orders again and receiving confirmation by teleprinter, we got our passes and warrants, boarded the truck and made our way to the railway station.

On Saturday afternoon, having had an uneventful journey, I arrived in Coventry totally unexpectedly, to be greeted by Margaret, Dorothy and the family, although the brothers-in-law were away serving in the Navy and RAF, the girls were all there and no Saturday working. Down the years they had had a rough time, air raids, rationing, damage to their homes, at least the horrors of war would be over, even if the stress endured still haunted them. My few gifts hardly made up for the separation, my daughter was to find a close relationship with me difficult to handle for many years to come. Margaret, had the tenancy of the house next door to her parents, which she was sharing with her sister and brother-in-law, an awkward and uneasy relationship for both parties, but eminently suitable to both, with such a housing shortage, and from the shared financial aspect. Like all leaves, you only remember the good parts, cinema visits, outings to the pub, and close contact with the loved ones, you missed so much when overseas, problems which I'm sure there must have been, were silently forgotten, and not referred to again.

The following Thursday saw a gathering of the crews at Melton, a couple not arrived had to be regrouped into other crews, I found myself again in the right hand seat this time with F/O Stenner, and W/o's Redmond and Swarbrick for the ride up to Renfrew. The briefed route was across to Liverpool Bay then north through the Irish Sea, passing Blackpool and the Lake District up toward the Clyde estuary. For July it was a strangely cloudy day and up front we were on 'our toes' being very circumspect in relation to possible other aircraft in the area, and the mountains in this part of Britain. Renfrew guided us in with homings, and the Liberator finally reached its destination. The ride from Melton to Renfrew took two hours, today it is done in a leisurely hour. At this aerodrome we were able to go round the hangars to see the fate of the aeroplane, it was to be converted into a passenger version, stripping out all of the arnament, turrets magazines. etc. Then after fitting seats in the bomb bay and other areas, it would be employed on long range repatriation flights to bring home the troops from the Middle East, and India. This work was being done by Scottish Aviation at Renfrew.

I'm going through this delivery in a bit of detail for it was to be the shape of things to come, bring an aircraft into UK, scrounge as much leave as one could then report back to Blida. The main group of the crews caught the L.M.S. Night Scot train leaving Glasgow at around 9 pm. for Euston. We reached the city of Glasgow at about six in the evening and took ourselves to a smart restaurant in the city centre, ordered whatever took our fancy and generally enjoyed the evening. On the crowded train we had difficulty finding seats but this was no problem we were used with roughing it, and after long flights coming back in a Dakota from Cairo, what was the problem with a few hours on a train. The train made its way through the night, stopping at various stations, on route, where some of our party got off. Carlisle, Preston, Crewe, until finally at around three in the morning it was my turn to make my goodbyes and step onto the cold deserted platform at Nuneaton in Warwickshire, about ten miles from my home. The first train out, to Coventry was at five thirty am, so with a long wait in store I curled up in front of the stove in the booking office and slept until the train came in, I turned up on the doormat, at my home, at about the same time as the milk, tired dirty, unannounced, and fit for nothing other than sleep. Before leaving Glasgow we arranged to meet at the Air Booking Centre at St. James's in London on Monday morning at ten or eleven o'clock, as most guys would reach home on the Saturday morning, it was another weekend with the family.

  The Air Booking Centre in St. James's St. was close to Cox and Kings branch of Lloyds Bank, and as many RAF officers' accounts were held there, it was a popular place to visit before returning overseas. At the ABC. we booked in as needing a flight to Algiers, showed our priority passes and generally cajoled the staff into meeting our needs, the place was very busy it seemed as if everyone in the city was in need of flying to somewhere or other. We, obviously as a group, were too many to travel on the same aeroplane, and I found myself with about twenty others, not all our crews, being transported by road, in an ancient, semi blacked out coach, driven by a man as old as or even older than the bus, to Lyneham in Wiltshire. Here to join a flight the following morning to my destination Algiers, in a Dakota of 525 Squadron. The journey was without incident, via Istres, in southern France and Malta, where we night stopped. Whilst admitting that the return flight was not direct, it took 12 hours to get back after six to seven going out. The route via Malta was to say the least a big detour, but I believe that Algiers was on the return leg. Maybe the flight was a round one via Istres, Malta, Algiers and back to Lyneham.

I had arrived in Blida, late in the evening of 19th of July and by the next evening I was back in Maison Blanche having replenished my bags, with clothes and money, in the meantime. This time I would be Captain of the aircraft, with F/o Bailey as second pilot and W/o's Dalby [Barrington' after the radio commentator], and Charlie Westerman, and again the flight was to be Maison Blanche to Melton Mowbray. Hectic wasn't it.

This time the flight was seven hours, I cannot recall any reason for the extra hour over the previous trip, maybe the winds were more northerly, it passed without incident. Only a case of monitoring the auto pilot, checking the fuel consumption and selecting full tanks on change over.

The staff at Melton had certainly mellowed now that the effects of peace time were upon them, it wasn't a problem to get a pass for the week end, and return for the remainder of the flight on the Monday following. For me it was a quick dash into Leicester by bus, followed by train to Nuneaton and Coventry. I was home before eleven at night on the same day. We didn't even get a bed or a meal before leaving. On Monday we took the aeroplane to Tempsford in Bedforshire to the east of the A1, the Great North Road, near Cardington the old airship site, from where the doomed R101 airship left on its inaugural but last flight, and Square bashing unit of this recent war. The crew decided to be at the Air Booking Centre on August 1st to return, this gave us six days no authorisation this time, we just took the time off, there didn't seem to be the bull of previous years. The RAF was top heavy with Senior Nco's. struggling to demobilise thousands of men, on to a jobs market that could not cope, where munitions and Aircraft production was at a standstill and the peace time roles of factories was yet to be defined. The friends I had still in civvy street were as confused as the service men, as to what the future would hold.

    I drove myself to go home, each time we brought in another aeroplane, on the reasoning that it was a wonderful experience to be free from discipline and regulation but all the time the skies called me, I loved flying. I was happier in the air than any where, and soon enough I would be denied the pleasure, unless I was accepted for a commission and if I were to sign on for further service.

CHAPTER FOURTEEN

This time at the Air Booking Centre, we were fortunate to be assigned seats the following morning from Lyneham, again with 525 Squadron. The bus waited for the passengers at St. James's to leave at eight in the evening, then going via Hammersmith, we took the Bath Road, past the site of Heathrow, which had recently become operational, and away towards Newbury and Marlborough until we turned into the gates of Bowood House near Calne, at around eleven thirty pm. It was quite a surprise to see the interior of such a stately home without all its trimmings, but being too tired to appreciate it at all we fed, and retired to our camp beds. At the crack of dawn maybe five am. we were roused with a cup of tea and wakey wakey. We were called to breakfast and a quick crew bus ride into the airfield at Lyneham about ten miles away, a short spell in the departure area, a visit to the loo I suppose and all twenty or so people, traipsed out to the Dakota waiting on the apron.

Life was getting more civilised as the autumn of 1945 came nearer, no more driving out to the aircraft at the dispersal, they were ranged up along the apron in the manner to be adopted on the civil airfield of the future. Transport Command was laying down the patterns for the new Civil Transportation service, BOAC had virtually been part of the command, and flew the routes to South Africa that the RAF. ferry crews had pioneered. The staging posts had undergone dramatic changes, even during the time that I was flying the route, at three major sites at Castel Benito, El Adem the field for Tobruk, and

Cairo West. The transit quarters were quite elegant, much use was made of the local stone for the building of sleeping accommodation, dining halls, and rest rooms, very cool in the heat of midday. In the dining rooms the tables and benches were of polished stone almost marble in appearance, easily cleaned and quickly available for the weary passengers, from those slow vibrating thundering Dakotas, where they were provided with the inevitable huge pots of tea and ready cooked meals at the canteen style window. Make no mistake the food was good, and after eating, if you were stopping for the night, there was an excellent bar cum lounge to while away a few hours.

On one special occasion, I had arrived at Castel B. and gone to the dining room for my meal, all ranks dined together when in transit, that's not to say that the officers were not treated with respect, it was just a convenient way to deal with the stream of itinerant travellers, going through the post, at any one time. When I sat down at one of the long tables with my meal I was next to a Flight Sergeant who was sitting with his back half turned towards me, I had to request if he would pass the salt and nudged him at the same time that I asked. As he turned to offer the salt cellar I recognised him as my cousin from Wallasey on Merseyside. Big surprise, he was eighteen months younger than me and had followed in my footsteps almost, all the way through his training. He said that his OTU. had been at Patricia Bay in British Columbia, where he graduated on Dakotas and was now with 216 Squadron at Heliopolis, Cairo. Some coincidence, I wonder what the odds would be on that happening? He eventually left the service and became a Senior Captain several years later with British Airways.

Another of those staging post stories, centres around a cold night, in early 1945, at El Adem. A group of our crews were on their way to Cairo west and looking for a short run the next morning, to get into the city early, we stopped over at El Adem, the place had been newly refurbished, the lounge was a pleasure to behold. A complete rebuild into a smarty airy comfortable room, we retired there for the evening and made a few purchases at the bar, then in a large semicircle around the fire, which was blazing away with the wood crackling and the flames shooting up the chimney, we spent a couple of hours, joking, telling yarns, 'shooting a line' etc. Along the hearth meanwhile, several of us had put tins of 'McConachies' stew, with the idea of warming them up for supper, of course quite a few beers had passed our way, and life was very comfy, when 'BANG' the first of several tins burst, no one had thought of piercing the tin before hand. Two more went off, before a braver man than I, rushed in and kicked the rest of the tins away from the fire, the stew was everywhere, on our clothes, in our hair, on the seats, the carpet was a mess. We howled with laughter, we shared out the remains and tried to clear up the squelchy mess from the furniture, while laughing until tears came to our eyes.

The bar man said to leave it, he saw the funny side of the occasion and made arrangements to have the place tidied up. Meanwhile it was all we could do to try to eat rest of the meal from the other tins.

The pattern of the flight back to Algiers, was by now getting to be stereotyped, refuel at Istres, in the South of France, night stop at Luqa on Malta, then fly on to Maison Blanche tomorrow. To Blida either a cadged flight of thirty minutes, or a crew bus ride of around an hour. What a sad sight Blida had become, fewer aircraft on the field almost no activity in the hangars, a general air of gloom instead of pleasure that it was indeed finally over, the whole war that is, since now Japan had been defeated.

All eyes were on the news bulletins and daily orders to check on who was to go home for demobilisation and when your turn might be. The Air Ministry or the War Office had devised some rule as to 'first in first out,' and many of the long service, [overseas] men would go first, rather as our choice on the first Liberator flights, back to England. For three weeks in August, there was nothing to do, other than make one's own entertainment, certainly the camp cinema got more up to date films to show, we began to take more interest in sport. Although cricket on a sun baked piece of Algeria wasn't a bit like the grammar school playing fields, however we did try our version of a Test Series against the Aussies in the Mess they were good but I think it ended honours even in the end.

Ray Godfrey had meantime got himself posted to Palestine to join his girlfriend from the time he spent at Lyneham, flying second pilot on Albemarles on the Azores run. Joyce had volunteered to come out as soon as the WAAF were permitted to do so, luckily for her, Group had a vacancy for a Pilot to fly the communication Beechcraft. They were eventually married in Peta Tiqva and 'lived out,' that is to say, off camp in an apartment, in the town, until demob. They came home in 1946 by sea, on the Mauritania, marital bliss only spoiled by the regulation that sexes were separated to differing parts of the ship. Oh, the staid Victorian views that still prevailed, even in the services, were not women so emancipated now that they had been doing skilled 'men's work' for the past six years? On one occasion at Nutts Corner, I had climbed into a Wellington to prepare for a navigation flight, and found an LAC WAAF checking the fuel state with a dip stick. She walked along the wing with all of the assurance of an old hand, and when finished came across to the cockpit window to give me the good news that we had full tanks, confirming the gauge readings. The point to this story is that I recognised the girl as one who had been at school with myself about ten years earlier. In peace time I met her again and now she was a Sergeant Airframe Mechanic.

Peace time was starting to look a bit grim at Blida, much discontent both with air crews and ground staff, also in the officer's Mess there were rumblings as to why things were taking so long to sort out. When the call to go home would be heard, who goes when, what to do in the meantime? There was no real change for the better, maybe the new government under Attlee might hasten in a new order.

I kept my hand in with a spell of instrument flying in the trusty old Anson, I shared two hours as firstly, safety pilot for F/O Bailey then, as pilot myself, here ended August, well almost. I was called to the Adjutant's office and informed to travel to Group

Headquarters in Valleta, for my Commissioning interview, on the 27th. This had come through at last, I had waited since March or April when I first applied to be considered to become an officer. I had realised what a fool I had been back at Weyburn in 1942 when I had answered 'No' to the question 'Do you want to be considered for a commission,' and therefore had applied at the first opportunity.

I presented myself at Group the next day all brightly polished, well groomed, and had an enjoyable interview with the Group Captain and A.O.C. of 216 Group. To me, although even now, somewhat apprehensive, as to what would be raised in conversation, what about my two 'prangs' would they count against me, the atmosphere was more of a friendly chat than a formal interview. All very pleasant and gentlemanly.

Interview over, the next thing how to get back to base? In the new transit Mess at Luqa I bumped into, literally, Mac MacKinley one of our longest serving Ferry pilots, and found he had got himself an old tired Baltimore to take to Blida, so with no further ado I was on the scrounge for a ride. What I did not know was that Mac couldn't refuse any one and that next day we took off with eight or nine bodies on board an aircraft normally crewed by four. The journey, although the aeroplane was crammed with bodies, was pretty fair, I remember that I stood in the rear compartment with two other guys, on the leg to El Aouina, where the ground crew nearly passed out at the sight of all these blokes getting out for a breather while the aeroplane was refuelled. Since it was normal to cadge rides back, there wasn't the same reaction at Blida on our arrival, as at El Aouina, just another bunch of those 'Ferry types' coming back in.

September started with yet another diversion for the unit. In Udine, a city in the north of Italy an inter services sports festival had been planned. From our MU. a group of athletes were to represent the RAF and the crews of 3 Ferry unit were to fly them there in two or three Wimpy's. I got the chance to make the flight in a converted Wellington. The turrets had been removed, and all heavy equipment, armour plating etc. and seats fitted so I was able to take eight passengers, with three crew.

A day earlier with 'Boots' Haley, I took the aeroplane up for an air test, found everything OK and signed her fit for the next day's trip. The first leg to Pomigliano passed without incident, we were refuelled while the passengers had a coffee and stretched their legs. Again in the air I headed for the Adriatic side of the Apennines to make a run up the coast where the ground crew amongst us could see the battlefields that the Eighth Army had fought over, going up the east coast of Italy from one river crossing to another. It was early afternoon when the port engine cut out, no warning cough just stopped dead, we swung into the emergency procedure immediately. It was about two and a half hours to our destination, the aeroplane was stable on one engine, but we had difficulty in getting the cross flow to work and were not therefore able to restart the dead engine. I was fearful for the safety of the passengers, this was something different to the usual. The pilot officer in charge of the sportsmen, came up to the cockpit, and he and I on my assessment of the situation, agreed that we should try to put down as soon as possible. The nearest airfield I was aware of, was at Pescara not too far ahead of our position. I therefore made preparations for the landing there, my wireless operator Charlie Westerman was a very experienced crew member who had climbed into the right hand seat to assist with the approach.

We made the correct approach and delayed the flaps until necessary, and contrary to the experience of Maison Blanche with the Warwick, I greased the wheels onto the runway as if there were no problems to worry about. We rattled along the steel plank runway slowing down to be met by the usual jeep, but with soldiers on board not the usual RAF driver, I thought this strange but followed to a tarmac apron before the tower. There was something wrong with the appearance of this aerodrome, not a soul on it other than ourselves and a couple of soldiers, I recalled that there was no response from the ground to my calls for landing advice. We climbed down the ladder to a warning from the squaddies that it was not safe to cross the open ground of the airfield but we should stick to the perimeter track, there were no RAF personnel on the site but a telephone was available. We called Foggia for advice, and also 4 Ferry unit to explain our predicament. Apparently there was an RAF detachment in the town of Pescara and the Army laid on a troop carrier Bedford lorry to take the whole group to the hotel occupied by the RAF.

Our troubles were recognised immediately, and a friendly F/o got things organised such that the passengers would go by bus through the mountains to Rome where they would catch a flight to Udine. That would be the day after tomorrow, as for the crew and myself we were to await the repair crew coming up from Foggia in two days time, meantime the sea was just across the road from the quarters and we were able to change in the room and cross to the beach and enjoy the amenities of the place.

It was on the third day that the repair gang arrived, I went up to the aerodrome with them to explain what had occurred and the action we took, this small team comprised one F/Sgt. one Cpl. and one Leading Aircraftman, all engine fitters. Having inspected the faulty engine, they found a supply problem with the fuel pump and the pipe work. It would be necessary for a replacement part to be flown in from Foggia, and they made the necessary telephone calls to get this done. All I and the crew could do was wait, we had no pressing engagements for the next few days, the sea and beach looked pretty enticing, the passengers had gone ahead we made the best of it. Not a difficult decision to make, we would stay put, with the ground crew and wait the outcome, our base had been notified and we were in no mood to go too far from the beach.

News came through that a ferry pilot would fly up with a new pump to replace the bad one, on the third morning. I went with the mechanics to the aerodrome and watched as an Anson cruised past with a side window open, and a crew member dropped a parcel out of the aeroplane. It bounced along the ground several times until it came to rest and was collected by one of the soldiers, driving the jeep. The contents were well protected by layers of old tyre and sacking. It was not until the sixth day after our landing at Pescara, that we were able to test the engine with the ground crew who had spent long hours under the cowling to change and repair the fuel supply on the dead engine. They had run it for quite a time and pronounced it fit for service, they made a 'daily inspection' as best they were able without a full compliment of tradesmen, and signed the Form 700. We left on the seventh day the 16th, it was still a mystery to us that the army were in charge, not the RAF, so it was question time again, what was the reason for not moving off the tracks or the runway? In a nutshell the grass areas were soft and there were no salvage crews to assist if problems occurred and in the meanwhile the RAF having no further use for the airfield, it was on a maintenance only basis and therefore closed to air traffic. That explained the lack of response from anyone by radio on our arrival. I cannot fathom why any other airfield controller in radio range had not warned me of the situation but there it was.

  Flying up to the airfield for Udine was a pleasant two hours over the sea past Venice away on the horizon, we crossed to the mainland and this time were delighted to hear the voice of the Air traffic controller at Campoformido respond to my request for landing information. They made us welcome, pulling our legs over the delay, and informing us we had missed the athletics, our other crews from Blida had had an enjoyable time with visits to Trieste and the lower slopes of the Alps. We managed a free day waiting for the sportsmen, and used it to visit the town. I cannot bring to mind anything concerning Udine.

  The following day, having gathered together our little flock of passengers and installed them in the aeroplane, we decided to give the airmen a further treat on the way back. We were getting a lot of flak about the last flight, ending in Pescara, but I heard from their officer, that in Rome they had a tour of the city albeit a whistle stop trip in an open RAF crew bus. My plan was to make Malta if possible before night fall, that meant a flight of about five hours and we were not leaving until midday, probably a close call to get there before dark. The run down the Adriatic was good in smooth air little or no clouds and toward the end as we were near Sicily, the start of a terrific sunset, which from the air was a new experience for the lads in the back.

There wasn't enough daylight to go on to Malta, and I made the turn in to Catania where I knew my passengers would have a fine time. The staging post mess here was in fine shape with good food and lodging. Sicily had been liberated two years earlier and relationships with the citizens of the island's second largest city were very good.

My crew and I refreshed our friendships with the staff, especially the Mess crew who would soon qualify to go home. It was several months since we as a crew had last flown into Catania, for our recent flying had been direct to Italy, further north as 4 Ferry unit had pulled out of Sicily and had been operating from Brindisi and Bari northwards.

After the night stop, we flew on down to Malta to give the lads the treat we had promised them. It was only an hour away so they would have a longish day in town if I could get the transport arranged. The planned stop was a success for all concerned, while the passengers enjoyed their day out in Valetta, we made the most of replenishing our supplies of ciggies and bottles from the NAAFI stores, after the essential visit to the paymaster, to draw our pay in pounds sterling.

Too soon for some, the time arrived to leave for the flight to Blida, a straight forward four hour flight, without incident mercifully, since I doubted if we could stand any more leg-pulling over the forced landing business.

It had been a fine way to spend twelve days on full pay and board, touring the Med with a great bunch of guys, who were always there to service our aircraft when the heat was on to get them delivered, maybe we repaid a few for the debt we owed them in servicing and repairing not only the aircraft, but also the inner man as the cooks made our meals for the long journeys ahead and the parachute packers for their care with the safety equipment.

The month ended with another of those quirks of fate!

Another Liberator due for delivery to the UK. and my name on it, together with nine other air crew, some for repatriation, to my favourite aerodrome Melton Mowbray.

CHAPTER FIFTEEN

There was nothing of great consequence on this flight until, of all places, on the final approach to Melton, all had been well, the call in acknowledged, permission to join the circuit granted, with the note '608, you are first to land' by some young WAAF voice from the tower. I confirmed my call sign '608 on finals.' At a close position to the runway, say half a mile out, the tower called '608 go round again,' I obeyed instinctively but for the life of me could not see another aeroplane on the circuit nor had I heard one on the control radio frequency. The abort procedure is not too arduous to perform, we roared away over the runway climbing out to one thousand feet and went through the drill again, downwind checks completed, tower responds '608 you are first to land,' flying the crosswind leg fine, all radio calls made and accepted, '608 on finals.' At almost exactly the same position the call, '608 go round again,' this time although going through the procedure I'm getting mad as hell, there was no one else on the circuit. I had three other guys looking out for the reason, it could only be another aircraft on the circuit or something on the runway, a vehicle or an animal. What was it, causing this disruption to a perfectly normal approach, hauling a Liberator around the sky was no mean feat, when you were fresh, but after seven hours at the controls it was hard work. For the third time I turned the aeroplane onto finals, called in, and waited for the reply as I continued the approach this time we were sure of our position and the state of things above, below, and ahead, sure enough she gave the same call, I was not a happy chap, I bellowed back that Charlie was bringing this aircraft in, that she must be blind, that her parents were not married at the time of her birth, that I wasn't to be intimidated by some jumped up little fart in uniform and keep out of my way when I got this beast onto the ground.

I put the aeroplane down in the usual smart manner we always did, the crew and our mess mates cheering their heads off, at each threat I made, to my tormentor, and taxied in behind the lead-in jeep with the 'Follow me' sign on the back. On leaving the dispersals I stopped the jeep when he reached the tower and made my way up the stairs to report in, the Controller had specifically asked for me to report to him, and not to the office on the ground floor. For some reason he was hopping up and down, on and off his high horse, as if there was a problem, he felt I should apologise to the girl in question, this I refused to do since in my book I was the one to warrant the apology, at no time had an explanation been given as to why I should abort the landing, and if he thought it to be funny, in any way, to play tricks on tired pilots, he had another think coming. I was threatened with disciplinary action, but I knew he was on thin ice, and I had a good case with my host of witnesses. I called his bluff and suggested he make a formal complaint to my commanding officer. At this suggestion, he promised he would do so, but I was too tired to argue any longer. I had made my point in no uncertain terms. I was totally dissatisfied with the attitude of all concerned in the tower, at no time before the incident or after, did we see any other aircraft flying on the circuit, and despite all of the recriminations as to disobedience of Traffic Control orders, I was adamant that the aircraft safety was not compromised and that I was preparing to make my own report to my CO.

There was no mention of a further flight for that aeroplane, to an MU. or conversion factory so, after a few days at home, once more it was down to the Air booking office and a return flight to base. Imagine our dismay when confronted at Lyneham by the prospect of having to travel in a Stirling, which had had, seats fitted and all armour removed. It was being flown by a crew from 46 Squadron and I would guess that there were about 25 passengers on board. Things started well enough as we climbed out towards the English Channel to cross the coast near Bournemouth, although the electric motors raising the undercarriage made a horrendous din, and the cold in the rear end was far worse than in the Wellington. Then the first signs of trouble appeared as we were near the French side of the channel, one of the starboard engines was running rough, and after about fifteen minutes was shut down and the prop feathered. Up front they must have been making provision for a landing at the nearest available airfield, we were not informed of the situation, what could we have done anyway? Between the coast and Paris the other engine on the same side was in trouble and shut down, now it was serious, and minutes later news came back that we were to divert to Villacoublay, a French Military field to the west of Paris.

Quite frankly, things were in a state of great unrest, in the back of the aircraft especially among the none air crew passengers, who looked terrified we tried to calm them but we were not confident ourselves as to the outcome, however we need not have worried as the wheels were let down and the pilot made a great landing using the two remaining engines, but on the strength of that one flight alone, no more Stirlings for me. As luck would have it, when we reported to the Air booking centre in the Place Vendome, in the centre of Paris, we were informed that there might be a delay in getting a flight to Algiers. They bussed us out to Le Bourget where the RAF had a small transit site for flight crews, the four of us remaining from the flight to Melton, W/os Bond, Cadman, Lewin and myself, were to spend, the next five days kicking our heels around the streets near the airfield, with visits each morning to the Air booking centre seeking a flight onwards, if we could get to Marseilles we could probably join up with a Dakota refuelling at Istres. No dice, I firmly believed that as we were not officers they didn't want to know us, and couldn't care less, so we had to take our own decisions, and find an answer.

It was soon in coming, one of our crew was talking to a F/Sgt. at the bar one evening and found that he was from the crew of a Dakota going back empty to Hendon the next day, and on the sixth day we were to be found reclining in the seats of a special Dakota of a very Senior officer, some C. in C. or other. Within an hour and a half we were back in the UK., thanking our Samaritans, and looking for a ride to the nearest London Transport station.

We flew out, ten days late, in the middle of October to reach our base very nearly a month after setting out with the Liberator for Melton, the journey back was by 167 Squadron, from Blackbuse, via of all places Paris, Le Bourget, to Pomigliano, then by 78

Squadron Dakota, to Algiers. The old base wasn't the same any longer, with so many of the old hands being repatriated, and all of the Australians pulled out by their Government, likewise the Canadians had also gone. The break up of the huge machine of the Allied Air Force was taking place, the like of which would never be seen again. Already on the aerodrome the old and crippled aeroplanes were being dismantled, or torn apart using tractors. Tales were rife of brand new engines being dumped out at sea beyond the harbour in Algiers Bay. Everything was being done to boost the flagging moral of the men, concerts, sports events, soccer matches, cinema shows, even dances. None of those were as successful as they should have been. Morale was low, more among the ground trades, they had had a long stint in North Africa, some from the very first landings, they wanted 'Home.'

With a certain amount of luck, I managed to get a few hours in, as safety pilot to a guy who was on an instrument flying practice, then one of those coincidences a Boston had to go to Egypt. I was given the job and two long serving crew came with me. The first day was to Luqa to visit our favourite island, for the last time maybe, we had a hilarious night in the bar with some replacement crews on their way out to Malaya, next stop of course was at El Adem. Not until after we had beaten up the desert road, between Benghazi and Tobruk at about a hundred feet, and nearly two hundred and fifty miles per hour, it was out of order, but the lads enjoyed the thrill of low level flying.

At El Adem the next morning it was a false start, I managed one circuit of the field with a very sick engine on the starboard side, a severe drop in oil pressure was the problem for the ground crew to resolve, which took a couple of hours, something to do with the supply line to the pump, then we were on our way. The delivery point was at an airfield called Kilo 40, the name was derived from the distance measured from Cairo, along the Desert road to Alexandria. To reach it we had to fly over El Alamien where the cemeteries were getting bigger, the German on one side and the Allied further along on the opposite side.

In town, in Cairo, we made the best of things realising that it was doubtful if we would ever come this way again.

In the Service clubs, and the pubs we used to visit, we made our farewells to those we knew. Many good men had passed this way, close friends and colleagues, even enemies, during these past few years, now to be spread all over the world with the job done at last!

Kaput! Finito.
Goodbye Digger, Goodbye Sport and you Canuck! We're going home soon. It's over. 'Ring down the curtain.'

Flying back in the Dakota from Almaza to Castel Benito, we played our last rubbers of Bridge on the parachute bag makeshift table, and slept as was usual, six and a half hours in a thundering Dak, was now becoming monotonous. On the way to Maison Blanche on the day following we flew over the site in the Algerian Mountains where a Dakota similar to this one we were in, had flown into the mountain side, while trying to descend through the cloud, miles from a safe location for a descent, killing four crew all South Africans, and twenty six of our crew members from 3 Ferry unit.

Poor navigation, bad let-down procedure, lack of navigation aids, and maybe a big dose of tiredness, all contributing to a very unnecessary loss of good lives, the one guy who got out, was the smallest wireless operator in the whole Mess, he was lying asleep on a stack of mail bags, at the main bulkhead. On impact, he was thrown out as the fuselage tore open like a sardine can. It was several hours before he came to, surrounded by a gang of Arabs who were looting the bodies of clothes, shoes and any useful kit, they could lay their hands on. Such a sad loss of life, does God decide these things? I don't pretend to know why. Not a gun fired in anger by any one of them, completely innocent.

Another episode was too horrible to begin to understand, the single engined aircraft were flown in pairs, to afford a degree of assistance to each other, each pilot took turns with the map reading and the aircraft were flown in loose formation. The danger point was when changing over the fuel tanks from overload back to main, the fighters had poor fuel gauges and on the overload tank none, I believe and it was necessary to time out the fuel usage. The point of this story is that two Mustangs were being flown toward Bizerte at a modest altitude when one of the pair had his engine cut out, he was not able to restart and turned toward the coast and prepared to bail out, however try as he may, he was not able to open the cockpit canopy, and despite all his friend's pleading to get out, he went down into the sea with the aircraft unable to save himself.

Some events were less horrific, but had their element of melodrama to add to the difficulties posed for the crew or in another case the pilot's dilemma when a crew member refuses to obey an instruction, and endangers the lives of all on the aircraft. A F/Sgt. who I knew well was on a routine flight to Catania in Sicily, delivering a Boston, the trip was as normal as any other and they were looking forward to the night stop, this was a popular place to enjoy an evening in the town and have a pleasurable hour or two relaxing.

Arriving at the circuit, as usual the pilot requested landing permission, and received the reply that it was clear for him to land but, and a big but at that, he was informed that back at Blida a nose wheel had been found on the runway and it was from a Boston, would he please lower his undercarriage and fly past the tower slowly so that a visual inspection might be made to check for a missing wheel on his aircraft, yes there it was a leg sticking down but no wheel. The first problem was to do with the Navigator whose position was in the nose section without access to the rear of the aeroplane, the Boston was only 'single seater' width, the navigator's hatch was in front of or beside the nose wheel bay, he would have to bail out. Not him, under no circumstances was he intending to drop out of that aeroplane, and that was that. The pilot had climbed to a few thousand feet to prepare for the parachute jump all the time trying to cajole the crew man to jump. He was adamant, not on your Nelly he refused, he would not jump. There was no alternative the pilot had to make a very careful approach as slowly as the aeroplane could and remain flying, the aeroplane came down beautifully on the main wheels and the pilot kept holding the nose up for as long as he could, rolling and rolling all the time with the front end in the air, until he reached the end of the runway where he hoped that even if the undercarriage leg dug in, as it must, the resulting damage would not be severe and no harm to the crew. The last straw was when eventually he lowered the nose the leg folded up, the aeroplane careered on, slammed through the fence and slid into a low railway cutting outside the perimeter.

The resultant prang meant that the navigator, who had had a terrifying experience, had to be rescued by chopping through the side of the aeroplane with an axe. Luckily for him there was no fire, his injuries were relatively minor and the rest of the crew were unhurt.

A terrific surprise awaited me at Blida. I was called to the S/Ldr's office to receive the great news that I had been granted my Commission, Pilot Officer at last. I was also told that following the usual practice of the peacetime RAF. I was to be posted to another unit forthwith. The higher ups decided that discipline fails if one stays on the same station as an officer, when one has been great friends in the Sgt's Mess. My stay at Blida was at an end, two days later I was flying to Naples to join 4 Ferry unit at Capodichino as a very junior P/O. although to keep the books straight I was entitled to a pay rise of one shilling per day, which on top of my W/o's pay made me almost the highest paid Pilot Officer in the service. During my last month at Blida, I had been investigating the requirements to qualify me for a return posting to the UK. on the basis of overseas service. It appeared that adding Canadian and African service together, with the service in N. Ireland meaning a break between stints overseas of less than six months, I could qualify to go home before the normal repatriation date. S/Ldr. Vivian gave me an 'Above Average' assessment in my log book. I had amassed nine hundred hours on the unit, almost four hundred as passenger returning from deliveries. I had delivered over seventy five aeroplanes, of around ten different types, not counting the different marks of the same aircraft.

I took 'Blondie' Scarbrow and 'Taffy' Redmond with me as crew to Naples, where we renewed the acquaintance with several of the 4 Ferry unit's crews who used to take on the aircraft from Catania, which we had probably brought in. They gave me a Hudson and my crew's job was to be the communications crew, taking other crews to various destinations, in Italy, to collect aircraft for delivery, or for us to collect them and return them to Naples. It was pretty boring stuff, stooging up and down between Brindisi and Bari and Capodichino, in winter and its bad weather with bods in the back with a war finished and no urgency any more.

This misery of a posting lasted exactly three weeks.

I suspect the Adjutant back in Blida had had a hand in the fact that on November 26th, I received my orders to return to the UK.

'Time expired' me?

At least when my overseas service was totalled up I had done my three years stint.

I dared not believe it was real, until there on the morning of the 27th standing on the tarmac was a Liberator ready for delivery to the MU. at Lichfield.

This time I was yearning to go home to my family, away from all the make do, and poor living, life on camp was no longer the fun it had been, the camaraderie wasn't there. Blighty was on everyone's mind, and especially mine.

CHAPTER SIXTEEN

The climb out from Capodichino, was one of the more memorable occasions ever of leaving familiar territory. The morning was a very crisp winter's start to the day, with a touch of rime ice on the outside of the aircraft, as we prepared to set forth, climbing through the early wisps of mist, playing on the slopes of Vesuvius to the east, the sun had cleared the shadow of the mountains and promised a fine day ahead.

Having been cleared to leave the circuit, I said goodbye to the tower and turned on to a north westerly heading to pass the isle of Elba on its western side and to the east of Corsica, the way mark was to be Istres on the French coast, where we turned to the north for the run over France. As we climbed from the Bay of Naples we could take our last look at Capri glistening in the sun, set in the azure blue of the Mediterranean sea, and Vesuvius still with a wisp of volcanic smoke drifting from its peak, back lit by the early sunlight.

On the control frequency I could hear another pilot, talking to the controller in Pomigliano, then I caught sight of him about a mile distant to my starboard, it was a Lancaster the first I had seen in the Med. We talked to one another, he and I, by radio, asking where we were each setting off to, and what our reason for being up there on such a fine morning, general chit chat, once frowned upon, in those days when security was paramount. He was on a trooping run back to UK with soldiers once the fighting force in Italy, now due for demobilisation into civilian life, with what ever it and the future may hold for them.

At around eight thousand feet, I turned up the turbo-superchargers, the Liberator fairly shot into the climb until I levelled out at sixteen thousand feet, a good height for performance and economy. We lost the Lancaster on the climb and although I occasionally heard him talking to control I didn't see him again. I like to think that we left him behind, but I'm not sure, we were at our usual speed of 275 mph. and could now see the Alps showing to the north and east.

Past the Riviera, Nice, Monte Carlo, and the sweeping bays of southern France, to turn over the airfield at Istres, on to our course for Le Mans, we were over the delta of the Rhone, the massive river running north to south through France to Marseilles. The run up through France saw the cloud begin to build up, and we were faced with a warm front to traverse on our track in central France. With the outside air temperature dropping, as we entered the cloud layers and the chance of ice forming, I began to lose height to find perhaps, a warmer layer of air where without too much cloud, we could continue on our present course without the dangers of severe icing that goes with cloud flying. Anyway, our safety height was now about four thousand, the Paris Control was forecasting better weather to the north west, and as our destination was St. Mawgan the Coastal Command aerodrome in Cornwall which was now becoming an important Transport refuelling and departure point, it suited me well to turn to the Brittany area and fly through light cloud patches.

This calling at St. Mawgan, was a new instruction brought in during October to force visiting crews to go through Customs and Excise, something that had not been required for the whole of the war, for the Services. At no time had we ever been required to declare goods, or currency on our passing through a check point on arrival at the staging posts or even on our earlier arrivals in Britain. Smuggling was often carried out by aircrew, but individually in a small way. Not in a highly organised way, and if there were any suspicions to be investigated, the Special Investigations Branch, [SIB], of the RAF Police would make them. Tales were rife in our Ferry unit, regarding various escapades, of running goods through the flight trails, especially in the early days on 'the Route,' from Takoradi to Cairo via Kano, Fort Lamey and on to Khartoum, flown by No. 1 Ferry unit based in Cairo. Their task was to bring up the reinforcement aircraft that had been brought out by sea in crates, and assembled in the RAF workshops at Takoradi and Lagos. They normally flew their Hurricane fighters in formations of five or six, with a Blenheim light bomber leading, whose job it was to navigate for the whole group, and was the only aircraft equipped with long range radio.

There is one story of a guy who ran snake skins down the route to Cairo on a regular basis, a nice little business, not necessarily illegal in the eyes of some and not offending the customs department of the country. There is also a story of a sad ending to one attempted run with gold, which was discovered when a package hidden in the wing of a Hurricane, was melted down after the aircraft crashed and caught fire somewhere along the banks of the Nile. In the wreckage was found the shining lump of melted gold, the pilot of course denied any knowledge of the matter, suggesting that the goods were put in by ground crews, and were to be recovered by the maintenance crews in the Canal Zone.

Along the north African coast the popular things were watches from Gibraltar to other parts of the Mediterranean theatre of operations. There were plenty of customers on the staging posts and squadrons for trinkets, jewellery and things too difficult to get. In the case of the watches, there was always the assumption that one could get to Gibraltar in the first place. Very few flights were destined for Gib. or originated there, with the one exception the occasional Walrus to deliver for the Air Sea rescue Flight or the Navy. Also the so called diversions practised by some singles pilots when passing through the straits of Gibraltar due to poor weather, who would go in on the pretext of avoiding the weather and refuelling in the process.

We had a chap in the early days at Oujda, who on his return to base would turn up in the bar with his small attache case and upon opening the lid, display a fine range of ladies and gents watches set out like a tradesman's sample case, all gleaming new in the light of the Tilley lamp on the bar counter. It was said he had a he had a healthy bank account in Cairo or Alexandria.

Another highly prized commodity was gold sovereigns, purchased in Egypt and sold off anywhere else in the Med, wherever the price was best. I well recall getting off a Dakota at Marble Arch airstrip, with one of our W/ops. who began scuffing the sand around as he got off the aeroplane and made no move to go to the reception hut for tea and some relief after the flight. When I queried the reason with him, he told me to keep quiet for the time being, until all of the other passengers had got off and gone to the rest room, whereupon he and I began searching or sifting through the sand at his feet, because he said a field dressing strapped to his thigh had become loose, and his gold coins had dropped to the sand. We found them, all was not lost.

On arrival at Maison Blanche, many aircrew rushed to the toilet block before reappearing on the public side of the aerodrome buildings, during these visits to the bogs, goods changed hands swiftly with a second party in the next cubicle, and before any suspicious party could connect the two events, the goods were off to Algiers.

On our way to St. Mawgan these things were not high on our priority list, the most important was how much leave we were to get and when we could reach home.

Approaching the south coast, I saw for the first time, the white waste dumps of the china clay quarries, they appeared as mountains on a moonscape so strange and eerie, foreign in fact after the interminable wastes of the desert, but not so unlike if you ignored the colours.

I circled over Newquay calling the control for landing instructions, and turned in for the runway making the approach from the sea. Not having landed at St Mawgan before this time, I was astounded at the size of the runway, it was enormous and gave no problems for landing, on this perhaps the last delivery flight of my career as a Ferry pilot. All was not over yet, upon leaving the aeroplane we were driven first, to the Tower to book in, then to Customs where they were intent on opening everything. Flight bags, parachute bags, cases, kit bags etc. In our now hard bitten attitude to authority we upturned the larger bags on to the benches in a heap of clothes, boots, flying kit, personal items, souvenirs, even 'issue' revolvers and left it for these 'keen types' to sort through, there was not a thing of value or restricted nature. We were just bloody minded after our seven hours from Naples.

For some reason we did not fly out the next day, and I expect that is the reason we were in the Great Western Hotel in Newquay that evening, remaking acquaintances with the town, not the RAF, the Initial Training Wings had long gone and the hotels that had housed us, in 1941, were back in the hands of their rightful owners enjoying, no doubt, the rush of holiday makers so excited at the prospect of this first post-war season at the seaside. It was not the real holiday season yet, and although November in Newquay is very mild, there seemed more bustle about the town than when I was here last. The RAF influence wasn't as great and people were smiling more, they knew things were better and would be more so in the future. Not many people can lay claim to having been on surfing parties to Fistral Beach during those war years as we did, when the sand dunes above the beach were mined, and we had to go through a roped off 'safe' route to the sea. I wondered when the mine fields would be cleared to make things normal again.

I also recalled visiting the firing range in the valley of the Gannel River, the only occasion that I ever fired a rifle, all twenty rounds in one session then never to pick up a weapon again in anger.

Four of us at ITW had even volunteered to clean up the bottom of a boat, used for Navigation classes, and repaint it, in Newquay harbour at low tide. It had been a diversion when we waited for our postings to a Grading school in the spring of 1942, it was a lovely time in Cornwall so far away from the war, but yet involved.

The final destination for the Liberator was Lichfield, to the Maintenance unit based there, a little over an hour away, which caused no hassle and was soon completed.

From the railway station at Lichfield Trent Valley, I was able to travel by train to Nuneaton and change for Coventry, getting home in about three hours maybe less from leaving Newquay.

Arriving at home I was secure in the knowledge that I was due for a month of leave, and a lot of catching up to do , the only instruction I had received was to wait for a telegram, giving my travel orders as to where I would report for further duty.

Meanwhile I had a wife who had patiently waited for this day to come, almost four years married, and only together for a few days at most, a daughter who wasn't sure who or what Daddy was, and felt put out with the stranger in the house, a big parental relations job to do there. And wizard stuff, a Christmas at home the first since 1940!

There were too many memories of Christmas's past.

From here on only the present and the future, would matter any more.

I had plenty of money to celebrate the homecoming, saved from long months spent in poor quarters and on rough rations in the Med. and as I've said before as a serving man one could do no wrong in the eyes of most people, the drinks were often on the house, invitations flowed in to visit and parties were the order of the day.

Staffy, the Wop. who had flown with me in 3 Ferry unit, had asked Margaret and I to go down to visit him and his family in Gidea Park, near Romford, in Essex. He had got a posting home from Blida just prior to my commissioning, and became an instructor at a Wireless Training unit at Desborough. He had promised he would take us 'up West' to see the sights, this would be Margaret's first visit to London.

My mother-in-law looked after Dorothy and allowed us to have a few days freedom together, it was as if we were on honeymoon. The time passed all too quickly, a stroll along the pier at Southend in December isn't too romantic, but we enjoyed every moment of our stay. Neither is going to a movie in Leicester Square to see an American film of Torpedo boats. Margaret's idea of a good night out. The title is etched on our memories. 'They were expendable.' The ladies were not amused and left, before the film was half over to walk around the West End and do some window shopping. The memorable thing for me was the fact that I was allowed to wear civilian clothes once more and made the most of it.

The family tried so hard to make this Christmas a good one, most things were on ration, toys were so difficult to come by, the women stood in queues for hours to get a few extra perks for their husbands and children. This was a side of life in England of which I was unaware. I had of course seen some during those Blitz years 1940 and 1941, what I did not realise that it was still the same, unchanged. My small contributions in the way of things from abroad, seemed paltry in the greater context of the real deprivation. In spite of plentiful work for both sexes and good pay, the things people really wanted were just not there and so the misery continued.

My mother had never accepted that I was grown up, and she certainly did not agree with Margaret and I being married, as for my sister, she was living at home with mother, as Eric her husband, was away in the RAF. They had a daughter a month old when I came home for this leave. Roy my brother had been in the Coldstream Guards but had to come out on medical grounds. My father was not at home having separated, from mother during the war. The only settled group was my wife's family, who had taken me into their hearts as one of their own.

Christmas came and went, it was great to be home, nothing untoward everything in the world was fine, until when the telegram arrived 'Report to Waterbeach' it said.

'Where on earth is Waterbeach?' no one in my circle of friends knew, the only thing I could do was to inform the family later after a trip to see the Railway Transport Officer. I reported to his office on Coventry station, he would have the job of supplying the rail warrant for me to travel, and must have the location of the RAF station in his directories. My wife would then know where I was to be stationed.

'Cambridgeshire' he said, when I inquired, 'Go via March and Ely, take the train to Rugby from here and change there, for Peterborough.' The journey lasted hours sitting on platforms, waiting for connections, travelling in dirty smoky, slow trains.

Later I was to learn the route through London, to Euston, to Kings Cross, to Cambridge and Waterbeach. But this piece of information was to be of little use, as my posting to 220 Squadron lasted but one month, January 1946. They were flying Liberator Transports ferrying troops back to the UK. I was adamant that as a captain on Liberators I should fly as first pilot. Not so, they, in the form of the Adjutant, were not having any of it. I was to be found an alternative posting if I didn't like the right hand seat. I wasn't made welcome on the station, I knew no one, I have no real memories other than dismounting from the train, at the level crossing near the camp on arrival in the late hours, on the two Sunday nights when I had returned from a weekend at home. I was not happy there!

CHAPTER SEVENTEEN

On the first day of February, I left Waterbeach for good, travelling through London, via Paddington and on to Newbury, where I changed to a little branch line train for Lambourn, up in the Marlborough Downs, famous for the training stables for race horses. I had to telephone for a ride up to the camp, on the ridge above the village, when the transport arrived I went to the headquarters of RAF Station Membury, to report to the office of the adjutant of 525 Squadron. They were the squadron that had taken so many of our ferry crews back to Algiers, on the return flights after their deliveries to the UK, during the previous year, although they were then based at Lyneham. Talk of coincidences and things going full circle. At least it was a Transport Squadron through and through, and flying Dakota's, not converted bombers. It was also now obvious to me, that I had avoided the fate which had befallen so many aircrew. I was to be constructively employed on regular flying for the present. So many lads had found themselves redundant and put to menial tasks while waiting for their release number to come up, perhaps several months ahead.

I found the quarters rough and ready in the wartime Nissen huts, of a second phase temporary RAF station. I was placed in a Nissen hutted site just off the road leading toward Newbury, in a wooded sort of hollow, the hut had been divided into four rooms each with facilities for four officers, we each had a locker for our kit and beside the beds an easy chair that had seen better service. The 'ablutions' as the RAF called the bathroom facility, were in a separate building with a muddy walk in store for those who used them. More often that not the water was cold I did not have a shower or any major wash job there, I was content to wash and shave from a wash basin provided by the bat man each morning in our room. If I needed more I would have to wait until reaching home at weekends, or even visit the local swimming baths. The walk from my billet was about a mile to the Mess, which in contrast to the quarters was quite comfortable, it was well furnished and the cooks served very good food, not that in the time I stayed there did I dine in the Mess that often. It was another half mile to the Headquarters block, the Squadron flight offices and the crew room. The very first job I decided was to get myself set up with a bicycle to ride around the site, as getting about was to become a problem at times, although in our room, of the four officers, we had three vehicles of some sort. Jack King had a BSA motor bike on which he ferried us down to the village pub, a couple of others had some ancient sports car of sorts, the difficulty with getting lifts anywhere, was for to all be at base at the same time, only if you flew in the same crew were the chances high. Then of course Newbury had more to attract us than Lambourn, pubs, cafes, cinemas. In the centre of the airfield site where two lanes crossed there was a country pub, with a name like the Dog and Gun, or some such country connection, it had the tiniest of rooms for the bar, and to see it crowded out with fifty or so RAF personnel of all ranks, all drinking and shouting and sipping at the same time, was a sight to behold. It must have been a gold mine for the landlord, right in the heart of the camp, the place was packed every opening time either morning session or night, there was little to keep me in the mess of an evening. I did not have many close friends here at least for the present.

I was integrated into the crew of F/Lt. Freeman DFC, who had F/o Harvey as navigator, and appropriately named F/L Nutt as wireless operator, our total flying time together before a route assignment, was a paltry one and a quarter hours. I was going to learn the duties of the second pilot the hard way, on the flight to Karachi. I did have a couple of days in which to spend time in the cockpit, with a copy of the Pilot's Notes from the flight office.

On the morning of February 14th, we left the cold damp fields of Berkshire, to fly south once more to the scene of many long flights, we reached Malta the first day with a stop at Istres near Marseilles, to refuel, landing at Luqa in the dark. We had a load of around 4000 lbs of hand grenades for delivery to Cairo Almaza, in crates strapped to the central panel of the floor, the seats used by passengers were raised and clipped to the sides to give access all round and for the crew to reach the toilet.

The next day was a two stage trip to Almaza calling at El Adem for fuel, and leaving the cargo at Almaza, where we stayed the night. From here on in it was to be new territory for me, for I had not flown further east than the Suez canal, during my Ferrying days in North Africa. My geography knowledge wasn't lacking, just the actual 'hands on' experience. In my youth I had read every morsel of information about flying from its infancy to the present day, and knew of the routes taken by those early long distance fliers, the landing sites they used, and which countries they over flew. What I was not prepared for, was the changeable nature of the weather as we flew over the deserts of Iraq. At first as we flew eastwards towards Habbaniya, on the main oil pipe line across the desert it was a fine day, as so often we saw in N. Africa, as we crossed the Lybian desert, the pipe line ran for mile after mile over the desert with pumping stations at regular intervals. It was after all a major engineering feat and the cause of so much unrest in the countries it traversed. Weather wise things became very ominous the further east we flew.

In response to a call from us, as to the expected weather conditions, came the reply from Habbaniya, that a desert sand storm lay ahead, and if we intended to land there we should do our utmost to get down as soon as possible. With around an hour to go we entered a cloud system at around eight thousand feet at the commencement of a let-down to the airfield. After twenty minutes it became darker and darker, we had the panel lights on, the navigation lights too, and it appeared to be raining heavily. Ten minutes later, it was as dark as night at around midday, we were flying on instruments totally, there was no sign of the ground, the sky, or anything for that matter, then the rasping noise began, over the sound of the engines, came this deafening, roaring noise, like shingle grinding its way along a beach, no one in the aeroplane felt at ease. At a further ten minutes, with an altitude of approx. two and a half thousand feet, we shot out of the leading edge of the sandstorm into blinding sunlight. Rising from the desert floor to many thousands of feet, was a red, roaring, swirling mixture of sand and air, high into the clouds it rose, up front of us was fine clear and bright, behind dark and foreboding. Air traffic control urged us to put on as much speed as possible, and come straight in without a circuit, to get down and into a hangar before the storm hit the airfield. We arrived in the nick of time, the jeep guiding us to the hangar, where the doors were ready and open. Neville Freeman taxied right to the door before shutting off, I thought at one stage he intended to taxi in. The ground crew pushed the aeroplane inside, shut the doors, and helped us to remove our bags, put us into a crew bus, then raced us across to the Officers mess, which was battened down to resist the storm when it came. Another ten minutes and we were in the thick of it again as the wind raged and roared, and the sand came through every little crack or cranny, it stung the eyes and got into one's hair, the bar was the best bet for the night. We were there for the night instead of Shaibah nearer to the Gulf where we would have had a day off as slip crew, for twenty four hours.

  The slip crew system was another Transport Command innovation, you flew the maximum allowed hours say eight, in two or three sectors, then handed your aircraft over to the crew waiting on the destination aerodrome, the aircraft went ahead with the new crew, while the recent crew rested. This gave the maximum utilisation of the aircraft yet allowing the crew their relief from longer hours in the air. It was also a very cost efficient way to run the system. It was the forerunner of the civilian systems of today. The next day early we set off with several passengers and some freight to fly the leg to Shaibah, we arrived in a couple of hours and slipped the crews, they went on, we retired to get a proper rest, have our laundry done, and eat a welcome meal. Unfortunately, we were informed we were No. 1 slip crew, and as such were on standby, this was bad news since there was no guarantee that the next aeroplane would not arrive that evening. Of course it did arrive at around ten pm. The next stage was to Sharjah, near Dubai, in the United Arab Emirates, as these Sheikdoms are now called, night flying for four hours, we were then faced after refuelling, with another stint of around four hours. It was extremely tiring and the effort to stay awake on the night legs, was draining of the senses to the point, that your imagination started to play tricks. The dials appeared strangely wrong as if giving out the wrong information, you could imagine that the aircraft was not on a level keel, the urge to correct a feeling of the aeroplane falling to the side or diving headlong forward had to be resisted. The sight of Karachi coming into view was heartening, in the pale light of the dawn we landed at Mauripur, the halfway point of our run, the day was for sleeping, but not before we had food and sent another load of laundry to the Dhobi wallah.

    At midday it was time to go for our carpets, we had been advised, or Neville Freeman knew were to go, as the four of us climbed into a gharry and raced at breakneck speed through the town to the carpet makers. It was so laid back, it was a sight to behold, on a raised dais around the sides of a square, we sat drinking cups of tea poured from elegant Victorian style teapots, while carpet after carpet was rolled out for our inspection. It was to difficult for words to describe, the sight and smell of these highly prized, hand made works of art. I'll admit I was out of my depth in this company but put on a brave face and chose what I thought best to suit our humble abode. F/Lt. Nutt had a stair carpet rolled inside his lounge carpet. Freeman had his own, plus a roll of coir matting for the Officer's Mess back in Membury. More tea and cakes were laid on as we waited for our packages to be rolled and stitched up ready for the flight home. It was also necessary for us to have proof of purchase for the Customs officer back at base, so one receipt for the correct price and one for the customs man, not necessarily the same.

    The ride back to the camp must have appeared hilarious to any onlooker, four RAF officers, a local gharry driver, and several huge hessian wrapped rolls of carpet all piled on the top of this horse drawn carriage, like something out of 'Alice in Wonderland.' We swept up to the gates of the camp and convinced the gatekeeper that as a matter of urgency we must proceed to the Officer's Mess on our transport and thereby saved the sight of us carrying the goods ourselves. Later that afternoon we were in the Ops. room being briefed on the return trip, we were to take 28 soldiers back to the UK plus a few mail bags, leaving at ten pm. The weather report was reasonable the only hindrance being a stiff head wind in the early part of the flight to Sharjah, and a weather front in the region of Shaibah. The crew bus collected us from the Mess after dinner, the bags, carpets and personal things were loaded into the aeroplane, the very same one we had arrived in, no further crew having arrived after ourselves we were the 'on duty crew' through the 48 hrs. that we stayed in Karachi.

With the complement of 28 passengers on board, with their kit and a blanket each, we prepared for take-off. Some of the soldiers were looking apprehensive about the trip, keen as they were to get home, the trust we had to develop in them was no easy task. All the talking in the world, does not breed confidence in those who do not understand what is happening or why certain things happen when they do, the various unexplained noises from the airframe and the engine roar are disconcerting enough to the RAF personnel, but to the men on the ground, the squaddies, the prospect must have been more frightening. Faith in the RAF was a first priority, and it seemed to fall on me to go to the rear of the aircraft to talk with them and hopefully answer their questions as honestly as I could. The general inter-service distrust was still there, but they were not able to hide all their fears, in this new flying business, fear of the unknown, did not bring loss of face, as it would in some other circumstances. Taking hot coffee round broke the strained atmosphere, and news of our progress up the Gulf was soon the topic of conversation, of course night flying for your first trip in an aeroplane was another difficult experience.

The predicted head wind had been correct and the aeroplane was battling against it to no great effect on the journey to Sharjah. On the way out we took three hours and forty five minutes on the leg to Mauripur, on this westerly leg we were forced to put down at Jawani, after three hours of bucking and tossing through the turbulence in the dark, to refuel. It had been a long tiring trip to get here on the border with Persia at the extreme eastern boundary of what in those days was still, India, we had expected a flight time of around five hours but at this rate of progress were in danger of running out of fuel. All disembarked, stretched their legs etc. while the ground crew called out from their beds, replaced the spent fuel, with full tanks of petrol, checked the oil levels, cleaned the Elsan etc. and made the aeroplane ready for the next leg, some four hours to go, almost twice the east bound time.

While the landing in the strong wind had been 'hairy' enough, the take-off was even more dodgy, because of the difficulty of manoeuvring on the ground and the heavy load to lift off. I had to admire the skill of Neville Freeman that night, an aeroplane loaded with troops, a high wind, and violent turbulence and the darkness of a night take-off at about 2 am. he was a fine pilot.

The weather front ahead was lying across our path at right angles to the track to make good, and from reports from Sharjah, at the line of the Hajar mountains which we would need to cross to reach our landing field. After almost three hours from Jawani, we were able to pick out the cloud banks in the lightening sky the early rays of the sun at this altitude playing on the peaks of the cumulus cloud at about thirteen thousand feet. A decision was needed now as the mountain range had a safety height of ten thousand feet minimum, and it was pretty cold in the back although we were using full heat, we of course did not have oxygen equipment, normally the Daks flew below ten thousand, where oxygen wasn't necessary. The crew would be fine, as they were accustomed to flying at height and also were very fit, but as for the squaddies, well we would have to wait and see.

We set the auto-pilot, and engines for a climb, thankful for the extra fuel and began, to ascend to try to clear the tops or at the very least get above the danger limit, at sixteen thousand feet there were signs of real distress among the soldiers so we levelled out heading direct for Sharjah and when over the beacon at the airfield began a steady descent first to the north to get to the base of the cloud over the sea and then turned onto a southerly heading on the radio compass to reach the airfield. This action was not without danger as it was necessary to time the period out over the sea to give sufficient a margin of safety to allow the return leg in toward the aerodrome to terminate at the aerodrome boundary, at around a thousand feet below cloud with good visibility. Thankfully we came through the cloud base at a relatively short distance out on the northerly leg, and were able to turn back in clear air, with the sight of the coastline ahead and the airfield not too distant. We were down on the ground shortly after, ready for breakfast and sleep. Here a stop over was arranged for the passengers and ourselves, but we were due to be off on our way, the following morning.

The sun was a bright ball of fire in the eastern sky as we took off for Shaibah, in Iraq, the Gulf shimmered like a blue carpet under the nose of the aircraft, and today there were no serious weather conditions to worry over. We were able to fly at a modest three thousand feet and keep the lads in the back reasonably warm. This was the first daylight flight since leaving Shaibah four days earlier, all the previous four legs had been at night. So the sight of the desert states along the coastal strip of the Gulf was interesting to me and many of the others no doubt, but it would not be fair to compare the aerial view and the experience of life on the ground, we were not privileged to have a choice. At last at Shaibah, we the crew, slipped here, and the men and aircraft, went on with the duty crew who had been awaiting our arrival. We turned into the billets after lunch in the Mess, then at around 2 pm. we had our heads down as some of our kit was sent off, to be washed.

The prospect of twenty four hours rest on the deck were to be shattered in no uncertain manner at around 9 pm. when an orderly roused us two by two in our bedrooms, we were 1st slip crew and the next Dakota was arriving in an hour. It was a case of rushing around, to find the kit in the laundry, have our baggage put into a truck, get the details of the weather expected ahead, the carpet rolls on to the aeroplane when it landed, and generally prepare ourselves for another night of flying.

We left at around ten thirty for Habbaniya, a couple of hours away, in another Dakota smelling of fuel and unwashed bodies, and rather dirty, the Elsan stank of the chemicals used in it, the loo was generally grotty with signs of someone's air sickness on the floor by the little sink. There were dirty sick bags and waste, in the bin, this aeroplane had been missed when the cleaners had supposedly 'cleaned' the machine at Shaibah, this 'couldn't care less' attitude was often found on some of these lonely outposts of Empire, but that was no reason to condone it, a report would have to be made at Habbaniya firstly, then at base on our return to the UK. We helped the soldiers to settle in with the heat on full blast and hot tea passed round, with a snack that had been prepared in the cookhouse. At least that was done right by the staging post at Shaibah, the lads settled down to sleep. Not for long however as the flight time to Habbaniya was only two hours or so, to drop the mail bags, collect the UK mail, add some fuel to our depleted tanks and get on our way.

Lydda in Palestine, now Israel, was the end of that night's task, still at least three or four hours away, and although the passengers could sleep not so the crews, the wireless operator tried to cheer us up with music on the intercom, but that probably made things if anything worse. In the dark of the desert night which I believe to be the darkest of all nights, the illuminated instruments reflected on the wind and side screens, the auto-pilot as reliable as ever doing the job so needed, by we two in the front seats, taking the strain of flying the aeroplane, we were getting to the stage when it was difficult to stay awake. In fact when I went back to check the strappings on the freight and visit the loo, I found the navigator already asleep with his head on his arms on his desk. Not as professional as I had first thought, these guys were some of the 'D-day boys,' taking in parachute troops and dropping supplies 525 Squadron had a great reputation, this was letting it down a bit. Don't speak too soon however, I was to monitor the beacon at Lydda, as soon as the Radio Compass would respond to the signal. The wireless operator did not reply when, I asked for the volume to be turned down on the music coming over the intercom, to allow me to tune into the beacon signal. Neville suggested that I should go back to the radio position and talk to the wireless operator direct. He was also asleep. Two down, two to go, and another hour or more before reaching Lydda.

The radio turned down I resumed my seat up front and got the station signal tuned in and set the radio compass. I had picked up a flask of coffee on the way back to my seat and for a few minutes we indulged ourselves to the rations and coffee, that the caterers had provided at Habbaniya. I turned the aeroplane on to the heading indicated by the compass and we both prepared for the last part of the journey. It seemed only a few minutes had gone by when I noticed that Neville in the left hand seat, was gently nodding away, to the rhythm of the engine's beat, and I'm sure I heard him snore a couple of times, surely he's not going off as well. It was bad enough for me, since I wasn't yet used with all this night flying, and the disruption to the normal daily routine but these veterans of so many arduous nights, did I expect too much of them? So there we were, a hundred miles or so from Lydda with the Captain and two crew members, plus all the passengers fast asleep, it was all my responsibility now to be vigilant and stay awake. I cannot remember if Neville had said to keep him awake or rouse him if he dropped off, but as we neared Lydda and needed to call up for landing instructions, I just had to shake him out of his slumbers and report our position to him.

From here on in, it was plain sailing we made contact with Air Traffic, received our instructions as to runway in use, the wind speed at ground level, and the barometric pressure for setting the altimeter, and began our circuit and approach, tired as I now was, I had a great feeling of relief to hear the tyres screech on contact with the runway and the slowing down at the end of it, with me 'tidying up' the aeroplane tail wheel lock off, flaps up, cowl gills open, booster pumps off, cabin lights on, for the soldiers, cockpit window open, a breath of fresh air at long last. At seven or so in the morning after debrief and report in, it was a good time for breakfast and a long kip, in the pit, after a good day and night's flying eleven hours over three legs and in a period of twenty four hours or there about.

Sleep we deserved, and sleep we got and took it. It was evening dinner before we raised our heads again. All this flying between Sharjah and Shaibah, then to Habbaniya and finally to Lydda, had taken place on one day the twenty second of February between about eight am. and seven the morning of the following day.

CHAPTER EIGHTEEN

The grim prospect of another night's flying, so soon after the previous lot, was scotched by Neville Freeman refusing to move off the base until first, the squaddies had had a proper sleep, the crew had a day's rest and the aircraft had a full pre-flight check. As it was the 24th of February, we were then due to leave on the 25th therefore we joined in with the party set for that evening in the Officers Mess, they had a pleasant enough bar at the base and room for all to prop it up while supping pints, and during the later part of the night I met to my great pleasure Oliver Large, the instructor who taught me to fly the Harvard, at SFTS in Weyburn, way back in 1942. He had stayed on instructing throughout the war and was now on his way to the Far East. I like to think that he remembered me, perhaps he was too much of a gent to say otherwise, we at least had a couple of drinks together, something not possible on the training station in Canada, he told me his aeroplane was a York, the variant on the Lancaster theme, that was to become so successful on the Berlin Airlift in just a couple of years time. After a great night of reminiscing and good company, we slept the clock round until, seven the next day and made our departure at about nine am. bound for El Adem.

The rest of the journey to the UK was without incident or if there were any I've forgotten them, night stopping at El Adem and Catania after two long flights over an uninteresting seascape of the winter Mediterranean, and a refuelling stop, once more at Istres. We had left Membury fourteen days earlier, on my wife's birthday the fifteenth of February. The whole journey to India and return, had taken a total of sixty hours in the air, over a period of fourteen days, and was done in sixteen stages. We had used more than 4000 gallons of fuel, many gallons of oil, drunk innumerable flasks of tea and coffee on this long trip. Our reward was the knowledge that we had made possible, the delivery of two tons of hand grenades to Egypt, and the return of twenty eight soldiers to England, after their time overseas, and delivered many bags of mail to the lads up and down the route.

In the Customs hall, in its new location close to the Control Tower our bags were opened for inspection, mainly as one of our crew had a reputation of moving things around the different routes, to his advantage, without payment of any duty, something to do with a large consignment of bicycle tyres or tubes the story goes. We declared our odds and ends, and showed the 'bills' for the carpets. Neville gave the receipts for the Mess matting to the Customs officer and we departed to our quarters to prepare for a spell of leave, we had an entitlement of fourteen days, anyway the carpets had to be delivered.

I have no recollection of dragging that large bale of sacking through the various railway stations, and the changeovers involved in getting from Newbury to Coventry via Didcot, change for Oxford, then Leamington Spa change for Coventry, finally I expect I took a taxi to my home from the station in Coventry. The pleasure on my wife's face at this surprise addition to the comfort, of our lounge was a sight to behold. It was a green woollen job with ornate flowers in opposing corners in many pastel colours. There was a square border of cream coloured weaving around the main body of the carpet with a tasselled edging of green and cream. It was I suppose, around four metres square and in England, where everyone had suffered all kinds of shortages for so long, it must have seemed priceless.

Now the routine of route flying would become the norm, whether it be passengers, or freight or mail, or a mix of all three. March was half over before I was in the right hand seat again, on the 14th I went with F/Lt Freeman to practice what we called 'free drops.' This entailed flying at around fifty above the ground at 105 mph. to allow the crew to drop to the ground personnel bags containing supplies, mail, newspapers etc. The RAF had not yet brought in Air dispatchers as air crew ranks, and the second pilot was to supervise the handling of the freight. The centre panel of the rear door of the Dakota, could be removed and brought into the aeroplane, then with a restraining strap attached to a harness around one's body, it was possible to approach the open doorway, to push the bags out, on the command of the pilot, using the red and green signal indicators, located on the bulkhead beside the aircraft door. Red to standby to drop, and green to push the goods over the side. It was a routine exercise that just required common sense and regular practice, all the crew were involved, since it was critical to get the bags away on one run, in if possible.

At the end of this training period, I was transferred to 'C' Flight, and became a member of the crew whose skipper was F/o Dick Sedin. The navigator was F/Sgt. Rice and the wireless operator F/Sgt. Tunnel, we were brought together as a new crew and our first outing together was to the Northeast German airfield at Schleswig. I didn't record the reason for the flight, but such a lot of our trips were associated with either moving people or freighting, usually bringing Servicemen back, on the demob run to Blighty. I do recall that many of the return trips to base in the early part of 1946 were in pretty vile weather, in the darkening skies of late afternoon. Our route over England was to the north of London to avoid over flying the city, then a small adjustment to our course when west of the suburbs. to align ourselves on the beam for Membury, always watching for other aircraft flying into or out of Greenham Common, just south of Newbury.

During March we made only three flights to Germany, the airfields at Guttesloh and Fullesbuttel, were the dropping zones where, mail bags, or bales of newspapers were the normal cargo, especially on the Sunday run when, we would be seen, sitting with the News of the World spread over the cockpit, while 'George' the auto pilot took the strain. At the actual drop site it was all go for twenty minutes. Dick and I would begin to make all the checks and procedures for the low speed run, at about five miles out, reducing height and speed, setting the flaps to give better lift, putting the mixture controls to rich in case of a sudden need for maximum power. When the run in at fifty feet was commenced, I would have to go to the rear doors and arrange with the others the readiness of the baggage, the removal of the door panel and await the lights switched by Dick up front. In fine weather it was an exhilarating ride with greenery flashing by just a few feet below, and on the airfield the RAF lads awaiting the drop, beside the grass area on which we would hope to land the stuff, first shot then no need to go round a second time, to complete the job. However when the weather was a bit grim, things became a sight more hazardous, the visibility or lack of would determine whether or not we would make the drop, driving rain is not the best of conditions and we might be required to make a landing instead, extending our flying time and making a late arrival elsewhere inevitable.

During our time off flying we, as a crew, would be in the 'Greyhound' pub on the London Road in Newbury. Mr. and Mrs. Pinchin, the landlords of the pub had adopted us, as if we were sons of the family. Provided there were no orders issued for us to fly, we would ride down the long hill into Lambourn to catch the GWR diesel railcar into town for a few pence fare, and arrive early enough to be at the pub for opening time. One of the attractions was the piano which one of the lads played very well and the fact that we had become quite good at darts. So much so that if we were available we played for the 'Greyhound' team. We enjoyed quite a run of success in representing the pub, in whatever league we played in. The crew also had a fictitious dog, which was of course entirely invisible to non believers, so it was customary to hold the door open a little longer to allow the 'dog' to pass through, and woe betide anyone who shut the dog out by mistake. 'He' was also required to sit at the feet of one of us and 'stay,' and would be scolded by one of the crew if he misbehaved. It was commonplace for our little group to be waiting for the doors to open at six in the evening, sometimes even for the morning session, when we would spend the afternoon in town at some cafe or other whiling away the rest of the time until evening.

Our commitments to flying permitting, we occasionally went home, for several days at a time, since our duty rosters were planned for quite a number of days in advance. It was as if we were in a civilian flying job, there were no fixed parades or reported duties, we occasionally had to do Orderly Officer duties, however I can only remember doing my stint once at Membury. We or most of the air crews, seemed to get up for breakfast, check out the Daily Orders, spend a leisurely morning up to lunch and then either disappear to Newbury, or even continue beyond on a visit to our homes. It was dependent upon having enough cash to travel by train or whether it was possible to obtain a lift, either by hitch-hiking or getting a ride in a friend's car who might get one on the way to the destination.

The problem with train travel was not having a rail warrant to cover the cost of the fare, finally this was resolved by asking for, when due for a warrant, one to cover the journey from Lambourn to, in my case South Shields. Ostensibly, this was to allow me to go to stay with my wife, on a home visit to her family on Tyneside. The next complication to overcome, was to pay the few pence to reach Newbury without having the ticket punched by an inspector, and thus reduce the holes in the paper rail warrant, since on arrival back at home we would press the paper with a hot iron to seam out the perforations. It worked that is the main thing, and was used for three or four months.

April was to be an interesting month in a number of ways, for instance we as a crew were to be involved in more familiarisation trips around Europe, visiting a number of airfields that we had not seen before. In the process of over flying the countries of Europe, I at least, would have the opportunity to see the terrible damage inflicted during six years of conflict. This was my first contact with the devastating power of the Allied Air Forces bombing campaign over Germany, the war in the desert had not left the scars on cities to the same degree as in Germany for example, it was as if in Libya that the battles had been on a chess board, the moves back and forth over the same playing surface, left no permanent reminders, just rusting hulks of tanks and artillery pieces. From the air Hamburg was a honeycomb of walls, through which one could see down into the bowels of the buildings, as far as the foundations or basements.

The purpose of our flights was to make radar assisted approaches to the runway, at each of the airfields on our prescribed route, as useful exercises for the inexperienced crews that we were at this time. Neither Dick nor I had covered the cities of the European countries on our travels and if we were to be flying to them it was to be helpful to be aware of the locations. As I remember it we had three complete crews on board and each crew flew a separate leg each day, but on arrival we made an individual circuit and let-down for each pilot pair on board. It was of no consequence whether the elements were favourable or not, we had the chance to see first hand the terrain on the approach and any hazards on the route of the final run in. I flew the initial course in and made the let-down through cloud if there were any present, all flying entirely on instruments, while Dick kept vigil for other aircraft in the vicinity, he would take over for the landing as we arrived on the threshold of the runway. The run-in to Berlin's Gatow airfield was a special occasion, since months earlier we had not dreamed that it might be our fate to survive the war least of all put down on the enemy's home ground, their capital's aerodrome. Years later I watched a film of aircraft arriving here during the Berlin airlift, and remarked 'I flew down that 'alley.' between those blocks of flats once,' the most unnerving part of the approach as you could look into the windows of the apartments as they flashed past the wing tips.

The first night we stayed at Buckeburg and went into town to dispose of the bags of coffee beans, we had each brought over from Newbury, for we had been told that coffee was a prime commodity for raising cash on the streets of Germany. I recall a dingy kind of bar or cafe I'm not sure which in the quietness of which one of our party acted as interpreter and obtained the best price, I would have thought that off loading the amount we took there it would have caused a glut, we had brought out seven pounds weight each in canvas bags provided by the coffee shop in Newbury. Suffice to say we were not short of money on that trip or for some weeks to come.

The next legs were flown to Frankfurt, Munich and Vienna. The day followed the routine of previous days without any hitch until we attempted to reach Vienna's RAF airfield in the darkening skies of late afternoon with some pretty heavy cloud around. This time it was to be a straightforward approach since the radar was not yet available, however it was first necessary to identify the airfield we were aiming to land at, and since there were three ringing the city, one each for the RAF, the Americans and the Russians, we wanted to be sure we approached the right one. The pilot on this leg called for assistance and when he suggested that the RAF fire a red Very light flare off, there were three shot into the air almost at the same instant one from each field. Great confusion, I can only think that the other parties thought we were in some kind of distress, however the wireless operator finally got through on the W/T set and was given courses to steer which were relayed to the pilot who brought us in fine and safely, after recognising his target airfield. The next ride was to Brussels, via Munich and Frankfurt, no big deal just another long four hours or so with one's feet up reading whatever news we had obtained, in Vienna or for those not flying probably sleeping in the back of the aeroplane. In Brussels we saw some of the night life that had emerged in this post-war Belgium, one of our party had been before or was briefed on where to go, so that we were in something of the order of five different night clubs or forces clubs during our one night stay. I reckon we saw the night through and had a breakfast in town before returning to the airfield, either that, or we were billeted in the town at a transit hotel, I don't remember which but the first story sounds the more likely. By the time we were back at Membury we had flown about sixteen hours and done the routes and exercises as was required of us all in three days or sixty hours, since we were on the deck at base my midday on the third day, quite an exhausting piece of training. Then back to the Greyhound once more.

To cope with the lack of flying it was normal as previously said to go home whenever it was possible, even this could backfire on one sometimes, as was to be shown in April and May. After the first two weeks of the month had gone by with not much in the pipeline as far as flying was concerned and a lot of moping around the mess or strolling through Newbury, I went home, hoping for five or six days off. Margaret and I had bought a tandem cycle to which I had attached a small sidecar, to carry our daughter, this was an inexpensive and cheap transport for the family. We often went for rides in the Warwickshire countryside, even occasional weekends away from home. Since the weather was improving at last I looked forward to some time out together.

This time it was not to be, for when I arrived at my home I was met by Margaret with her bags packed ready to leave and insisting we go back to Newbury post haste. I believe I had time for a cup of tea but that was all, then it was back to the railway station to take an early evening train, it must have been luck that we reached Newbury in time to find a hotel with a room vacant, however after a telephone call to likely places we got fixed up at the Chequers on the Bath Road. This was heaven for both of us, the first time as husband and wife we had the chance to be free of family relations and have what amounted to a honeymoon. It was a Thursday night that we arrived at the hotel and whenever possible Margaret wanted to walk the length of the High street so that the other ranks would salute me on the way through. It made her feel proud of the fact that her chap was an officer. It was so embarrassing and I protested strongly, she just saw it as a joke, but to us officers it was something that occurred each day and was not sought after. At breakfast on the Saturday morning the manager asked if we were leaving that day as he had booked a rugby football team in for the weekend and needed our room. Lady Luck was on our side that Saturday afternoon for on enquiring at the Hatchet Hotel in the Market Place, we were offered a room on the top floor overlooking the square, a great vantage point.

That evening Dick came into town with the news that we were due to fly on Monday morning, so much for a few days off. It wasn't too much hassle because things were straight forward Buckeburg and return, cargo out and passengers back. The month ended with a delivery of a Dakota from Kemble to Honnington. Each evening I was able to travel into town on one of the trucks and return to the hotel in effect I was ostensibly living out authorised or not, I spent the next week flying into Germany by day, and returning to town tired out most nights. Whilst Margaret was enjoying her stay the countdown had commenced to the day of demobilisation for me, I now was aware of the date that my service would cease in the RAF. July 16th 1946.

First there was the matter of a series of flights with F/Lt. P----- to Hamburg in a Dakota with full passenger seating where I saw at first hand the damage that had been done to the nervous system of a great pilot, we were approaching the airfield at Hamburg, through a frontal system at a good height and had the need to fly down on a GCA approach. He developed a twitching action in his neck, and ordered me to fly the radar approach through the cloud. I talked all of the way down with the controllers, the skipper and I made all the right moves in the procedures but all of the way down through that mass of cloud he was as nervous as a cat, then when I brought the aeroplane through the cloud base at around three hundred feet, he took over the visual flying, as correct procedure and landed without a problem and no sign of his previous twitching. I believed it to have been the result of many hours of operational flying in difficult circumstances, probably in unarmed transport planes.

We had several high ranking people on board these last few flights and we were using the old Croydon airfield too for departures and return arrivals, for the final flight was Croydon to Nuremburg and return, question were the passengers to do with the Nazi trials? We will never know.

The RAF were not over generous with their praise ratings, after almost two hundred hours flying in the right hand seat from early February to mid June, about three months, the best the Wingco. Flying could muster up was as a transport co-pilot AVERAGE I felt deprived of any dignity. The last entries for 'total flying to date' show that throughout my war service I had flown one thousand and seven hours in the pilot's seat and almost five hundred hours as a passenger mainly in the back of the Dakotas, but no more, next stop Uxbridge and a civvy suit, raincoat, and trilby hat. That was my war, but not the last of my flying for the RAF and my country.

CHAPTER NINETEEN

The years between 1946 and the Korean war were a readjustment period, very painful to the ego, and the learning of new routines, totally divorced from the service life that I had lived for the previous five years. Then, the state of a married life had depended on a kind of correspondence course of letters, to an fro via the forces postal network. When fortunately the postings dictated a journey via the home town or at the least within a short distance it allowed the occasional visits to spend a short time together. It had been less than ideal, the changed demand on my emotions, trying to understand a relationship for which there is no training, but the hard school of life and the need to come to terms with the reality of providing for my family. Throughout these years I had a leisure activity of serving on the RAF Volunteer Reserve, the equivalent of the Territorials, which as well as giving pleasure in flying once more, also provide a much needed extra income. I was appointed to a commission in the General Duties Branch of the reconstituted Royal Air Force Volunteer Reserve, on the 21st of March 1949 as a Pilot retaining the rank of Flying Officer, having first to relinquish the commission I held in the wartime RAFVR. The appointment was for a period of five years and my unit was the No 7 Reserve Flying School, Desford in Leicestershire, having passed another tough medical I was found fit to fly. The letter from the Air Ministry granting my commission also expressed the appreciation of the Air Council for the services I had rendered to the Royal Air Force during the period of national emergency and granted me permission to retain the rank of Flying Officer and my personal number 200896.

Ray Godfrey and I were to meet again in our home town, the post-war Coventry, smashed and battered by Hitler's bombers and in need of a major repair job. I returned to my former occupation as a draughtsman in a local structural engineering firm, the pay was poor, the office conditions not good but it was a case of earning to feed our little family which had a new member in the May of 1947, when our second daughter Pamela was born. My tasks at work were varied and the learning curve was steep. I had been away too long I wasn't interested in the repair of bombed buildings, fitting new roofs to semi derelict shops or factories. I hated the trips out to measure for a Dutch barn for some farmer or other in a countryside to which I was a foreigner, my sights were more on the new to replace the old. Ray had gone back to his old firm where he serviced and maintained the machinery in a lingerie factory, meanwhile he had bought himself a Triumph twin motor cycle and I had got hold of a second hand BSA motor cycle and sidecar. It was on these machines that we would travel to Desford in Leicestershire to attend our evening classes once per week, usually Thursday and at weekends for our flying sessions, until we learned that the petrol ration coupon allowance, and mileage expenses were better in favour of having a motor car rather than the motor cycle. The bikes had to go and then the wangle of travelling together in one car, rather than in two, came into being, culminating in later years in car loads of up to five chaps all on the same fiddle over petrol and cash. He bought a Wolseley and I a Standard.

They served us well for three years clocking up the miles come hell or high water travelling the twenty miles or so each way.

As weekend fliers we began to rack up the hours especially since our pay was based on attendance on a daily basis. It was reckoned that we were able to earn an extra week's money per month. Then of course a commitment had to be made to do 14 days annual training full time on the site, usually living out at home, but enjoying the comforts of the Mess when on the camp. There were often opportunities to make cross country flights to other reserve schools, in fact it was probably a well rehearsed ploy on the part of our instructors to send those on annual training on these excursions to get them out of their hair and continue to explore the easy life, for in summer it was certainly easy. They were employed by the civilian firm of Reid and Seagrist and held RAF ranks on the reserve, the company contracted to provide the aircraft and training to the RAF, who financed the whole thing. These cross country exercises were gentlemanly events no flight much greater than about an hour, say to Cardiff or Rochester where on arrival the local RFS would certainly invite one to lunch in their mess displaying the right level of hospitality, on a fine day, perhaps a lounge in the sun beneath the tower while the mechanics serviced and refuelled the aeroplane. As for the rest of the day, a leisurely flight back to base and tea, what a life!

At Desford we had Tiger Moths to fly, not as exciting as the Auxiliary Airforce with their modern aircraft but at least we had the chance to maintain and practise our skills, and of course we had many hours of experience to fall back on. In fact it was noticeable how many of the reservists wore their medal ribbons and the numbers of DFM's and DFC's there were in the ranks of the RAFVR. It was always solo flying that we did, other than the check dual flights with the instructors, at no time were reservists to fly in the same aircraft, but I have memories of going to various air shows with 'Bats' Bullmore the senior of the instructors to put on a display of aerobatics which frankly I would have thought impossible in a Tiger, if I had not been in the aeroplane with him, the rolling and looping that he did was out of this world, the G-forces applied had to be endured to be believed.

Two years after enrolling and enjoying the garden party type of atmosphere on the reserve school, especially on those hot summer days when after flying we were able to relax on the veranda of the Mess for a few drinks and a chat in the lingering evening sunset, the war in Korea began and the Air Force realised that they were short of experienced pilots, and the need for reserve pilots to upgrade their knowledge on the latest thinking. plus training the men they had, in up to date advanced techniques. The Auxiliaries were on standby some in their jet powered aircraft, and the VR's were still on Tigers or if lucky on Chipmunks, the need for further experience in the latest techniques was very apparent. It was for these reasons that Ray and I were called back to the service in mid December 1951, I was posted with at least one other from Desford to RAF Finningley in Yorkshire. Ray went to Ternhill, where in all its wisdom the RAF once again excelled itself in putting a square peg into a round hole, all of Ray's flying except for Tiger

Moths had been on heavy twins. At Ternhill they were to teach him to fly Spitfires to be followed by Vampires. For us at 101 Reserve Flying School Finningley, it was a case of a different aircraft again, this time the Airspeed Oxford for a session of mainly instrument flying to obtain a category of competency, for flying on instruments. This would be dictated by the minimum weather conditions in which one was allowed to fly, type of weather, cloud base, height, visibility etc. and how the pilot coped with the conditions. The level achieved in the flying test would set the rating given. I must have had a good day at the time I was assessed, for I was given a Master instrument rating, the top grade. Most of our intake were from Bomber command or Transport, and ninety per cent of them attained the top rating.

We had some very experienced pilots among our group, one chap with two tours on Wellingtons and one on Lancasters, another couple were ex Transport Command on Dakotas, having been in on the Armheim drop and resupply flights. George was a friend from Desford who had been called up like myself, he had been on a transport squadron, supply dropping and trooping from UK into Germany, and he lived in Hinckley on my route to Doncaster. I would collect him on Sunday afternoons to travel to Finningley, he not having a car shared the expenses with me, we travelled home each Friday night and in winter in those old cars it was some feat on certain days when icy or foggy, as we used to dash up the A46 and A614 roads to Bawtry then into the aerodrome at Finningley.

My companion sharing the room, was Jack Bretherton from Liverpool he was an ex B25 Mitchell pilot who had seen plenty of action on low level operations during and after the D-Day landings. There were fourteen pilots on No. 10 course a sensible number, who shared the duties of first and safety pilot between each other and were also grouped in pairs with the same instructor, mine was a Welshman called Sgt. Oliver Thomas who seemed to spend most of the time in the air trying to get me to sign on for a short term engagement, there was the inevitable snag though we could not bet on receiving a commission, I was only guaranteed a F/Sgt. or equivalent, no good. It was quite interesting to discover the number of hours the instructors had accumulated on the Wellingtons that they were to teach us to fly, most of the reservists who had flown the aircraft had many hundreds of hours on the type. Olly Thomas had only about fifty hours total time instructing on the Wimpy, however he was able to put me right on single engine flying procedures so much so that one day I was doing landings one after another with one propeller feathered, mistakenly believing that was the order for the practise that day. The Wing Commander in charge of Flying was in the Control tower at the time, and I received orders to terminate flying and report to him on landing. Whilst I pleaded that the orders were specific, he disagreed and tore me off a strip in front of everyone in the room much to my embarrassment. The point was that I had gained useful experience in the process despite breaking the rules, I also found on this refresher course that the Wimpy was more agile than I had known during the war admittedly the models we were using were without any armour or weaponry, turrets etc. and in consequence were much livelier in response to the controls.

The flying programme was quite intense for we were on the Wellington section for only six weeks. Five days each with all weekends off, real civvy street stuff, and in that time we made several cross country flights both by day and night until at the end of the course I was showing seventy-hours total on the Wimpy with twenty of them night flying, then of course there was the Oxford instrument flying, a total of thirty hours of which fifteen were in the blind flying mode, doing beam approaches or Ground controlled approaches called GCA's. That blind flying was some of the hardest work I ever did in the air, the demands on concentration were huge.

There was a sad incident during our time there. His Majesty the King died and we were called to a parade to recognise the fact and to honour the accession of Queen Elizabeth to the throne.

There was a funny side to the news however, since on landing after a session of circuits and landings, I was greeted by someone from the flight office who said that King is dead, my immediate reaction was George King, my friend from Desford, had pranged, which gave me quite a turn, since we did not expect accidents at least not fatal ones in peace time.

Another coincidence was meeting an old friend who served with me at Newquay back in 1941, he also had trained on Wellingtons and then transferred to Stirlings, with which he had towed gliders for various drops associated with the Normandy landings and others in the South of France, over the Vichy sector.

Again on one of the dining-in nights, a fresh face appeared in the Officers Mess sitting opposite to me and I was sure that I knew the chap from somewhere in the Service, it was a surprise to learn that he was ex. F/Sgt. Wright who had served on 3 Ferry unit at Blida with me, although he flew the single seater fighters. He had just come in that afternoon from Pershore with a Meteor jet fighter for the auxiliary squadron based here at Finningley.

I quizzed him with regard to how he had spent his time since last we were together in the sergeants mess, eight or more years ago. He explained that he had signed on for further extensions to his service in two year stints, until he was finally accepted for a short service commission.

Our course came to an end without ceremony and nothing to show in our log-books other than our instrument ratings, we were not to be used in a combat role and returned to our reserve units.

The school at Desford had received new aircraft, the Percival Prentice, a single engined side by side, two seater trainer more advanced than the Tiger Moths which had been given over to primary training for new regular trainee pilots being taught to fly on the same field as ourselves. Things could get a little congested at times, and being a grass aerodrome you had to watch the direction of others as well as yourself.

David Abercrombie and I were to begin a course as flying instructors in the Prentice aeroplane taking turns as the pupil or the instructor, when we put into practice those things we had learned with the full time instructor. This was a fruitful time for both of us, the experience gained was encouraging us to better flying habits and a greater sense of discipline. We were even given the opportunity to teach ATC cadets the rudiments of flying when they came for their air experience sessions. Life was truly pleasant at this time.

To us on the reserve it was a flying club atmosphere, pop in for a flight whenever passing or drop in to the mess for a drink or friendly evening, we also had family occasions such as a Christmas party for the children of the members. At these functions the catering staff put on a great tea for the children and Santa in the form of Sgt. Fieldhouse one of the instructors arrived by aeroplane a DH Dominie twin biplane, the French doors leading out to the veranda were open for the children to see Santa arrive and they rushed out to meet him as he turned into the drive in a jeep.

It was a sad ending to flying for many of the Reservists in 1953 when the Air Ministry just shut down the RAFVR. No reason given, no formal notice, just to arrive one day and be told 'Its finished.' The entries in my log-book simply peter out, no summary or final statement of all those years of effort, as if I had withered away and disappeared into the mists of the past.

The memories of those wonderful days, high in the blueness of the earth's heaven, are some of the most vivid, I hold in three score and ten plus years of experiences I have passed through, in my passage on this fair earth of ours. I have navigated over about a half of the northern hemisphere and since leaving the RAF and piloting aeroplanes, I have continued to explore more countries and flown 'up front' in the cockpit of modern jet-liners when ever the occasion allowed. I have flown higher further and faster than ever before but the memory of those years in the Service are as clear as yesterday. From Tiger Moth and Magister to Concorde I'm proud to have been part of this Century, and of its aviation history.

Charles